Captain Bączkowski's extraordinary memoirs, those of a young Polish cavalry officer, covers his life story from childhood to his great wish of becoming a cavalry officer being fulfilled a few years before the outbreak of the Second World War. His idyllic life was shattered by the German invasion on 1 September 1939. The crux of the memoirs are his wartime experiences during the Polish 1939 Campaign when he commanded a bicycle platoon in the 19th Lancers Regiment, taking part in the well-known Battle of Mokra when the Volhynian Cavalry Brigade held up a German Panzer Division. Following the fall of Poland, he escaped across the mountains into Hungary from whence to France to join the reforming Polish Army. After the collapse of France, he was evacuated with the remnants of the Polish Army to Britain to continue the fight against Nazi Germany. He saw service in Scotland and then joined the British Army in West Africa as part of a scheme where 273 Polish officers received short time commissions in the British Army. On his return to the Polish Army he was posted to the 1st Armoured Division and took part in the North West Europe Campaign. His story ends with his decision to remain in exile after the Soviet takeover of Poland in 1945, service with the Polish Resettlement Corps and first tentative steps in creating a new life in London. His love of horses forms a continuous theme throughout his life.

On 2 March 2007, Dariusz Szymczyk was awarded the Gold Badge of the Polish 1st Armoured Division for his work in promoting the history and traditions of the Division. He received his MA in History from the University of Gdańsk. Having completed his doctoral studies, he is now preparing a thesis on *Soldiers' routes to the Polish 1st Armoured Division 1939-1947*. Dariusz Szymczyk also works as a volunteer at the Polish Institute and Sikorski Museum in London.

Barbara (Korwin-Kamieńska) Herchenreder is a British-born native speaker of both English and Polish, with 35 years of experience. She is a retired lecturer on post-graduate courses in Bi-lingual Translation (University of Westminster), Technical Translation (Imperial College of Science, Technology and Medicine) and specialises in historical and military material. Barbara Herchenreder has been awarded the Polish 'Pro Memoria' medal for contribution to the preservation of Poland's heritage.

IN PEACE AND WAR

Memoirs of an Exiled Polish Cavalry Officer

Tadeusz Bączkowski

Captain Tadeusz Bączkowski in a pre-war Polish uniform (painted
by Halina Karska, 1979). *(Dariusz Szymczyk Collection)*

IN PEACE AND WAR

Memoirs of an Exiled Polish Cavalry Officer

Tadeusz Bączkowski

Compiled and edited by Dariusz Szymczyk

Translated by Barbara Herchenreder

Helion & Company

Helion & Company Limited
Unit 8 Amherst Business Centre
Budbrooke Road
Warwick
CV34 5WE
England
Tel. 01926 499 619
Fax 0121 711 4075
Email: info@helion.co.uk
Website: www.helion.co.uk
Twitter: @helionbooks
Visit our blog http://blog.helion.co.uk/

Published by Helion & Company 2019
Designed and typeset by Farr out Publications, Wokingham, Berkshire
Cover designed by Paul Hewitt, Battlefield Design (www.battlefield-design.co.uk)
Printed by Hobbs the Printers, Totton, Hampshire

Translation from the Polish language to English financed by The Foundation of the Polish Ex-Combatants
Association in Great Britain and the Polonia Aid Foundation Trust.

Our grateful thanks go to Jan Wojciech Bączkowski for permission to publish an English language version of his
uncle's memoirs.

Originally published in Polish under the title: *Jak dojechałem do tej stumetrówki. Wspomnienia ze służby wojskowej*
[*lit.* How I reached my Hundredth Milestone. Memoirs of my Military Service] © Gdańsk University. Polish
edition published by Gdańsk University Publications, ISBN 978-83-7865-475-9.

Text of English edition © Barbara (Korwin-Kamieńska) Herchenreder 2018
Photographs © as individually credited
Map © Helion & Company 2018

ISBN 978-1-912866-01-4

Front cover: The Polish 1st Armoured Division in Normandy, early August 1944. The first briefing at Divisional
HQ. Seated from the left are: Capt. Kamil Czarnecki, Capt. Leon Czekalski, Maj. Michał Wąsowicz, Anon., Col.
Kazimierz Dworak, Maj-Gen. Stanisław Maczek, Maj. Ludwik Stankiewicz, Maj. Stanisław Snarski. Standing
from the left are: Lt. Tadeusz Bączkowski, Lt. Zygmunt Fudakowski, Capt. Tadeusz Wysocki. (Courtesy of the
Polish Institute and Sikorski Museum). Back cover: Bronze cast of a horse by Stefan Przywóski. (Dariusz Szymczyk
Collection)

British Library Cataloguing-in-Publication Data.

A catalogue record for this book is available from the British Library.

For details of other military history titles published by Helion & Company Limited contact the above address, or
visit our website: http://www.helion.co.uk.
We always welcome receiving book proposals from prospective authors.

Contents

List of Photographs and Map

Setting the Scene

A Foreword by the Translator

Barbara (Korwin-Kamieńska) Herchenreder

Poland's history down the centuries is a tale of great victories and painful defeats. Once a mighty power stretching from the Baltic in the north to the Black Sea in the south, then a nation and a state partitioned by its neighbours. The period of the three Partitions – by Prussia, Austro-Hungary and Russia – at the end of the 18th Century erased Poland from the map of Europe but not from Polish tradition and yearning for independence. This was a time of dramatic uprisings against the oppressors, all of which ended in tragedy. Yet the spirit of the Poles remained unbroken.

A common thread running through Poland's history is the Poles' love of horses and the romantic picture of the Cavalryman, or Uhlan (Lancer). Poland's cavalry did, indeed, contribute to many victories – perhaps the most famous being the Battle of Vienna in 1683 which led to the fall of the Ottoman Empire. Here, the might of the Polish heavy cavalry, the Winged Hussars, led by King Jan Sobieski, bore down on the enemy, the wind whistling through the feathered 'wings' of the Hussars' armour. A dramatic and colourful picture, the pride of every Pole! Surely every little Polish boy has played with figures of winged hussars. Then came the exploits of the Polish Uhlans in Napoleon's army, resplendent in their navy and amaranth coloured uniforms and high 'chako' hats. There have been countless songs sung about these daring young men on their beautiful horses, sabres in hand, ready to do battle or to melt the heart of many a maiden! The Polish Legions, established during the First World War, had their fair share of dramatic exploits by Polish cavalrymen, gathered from the armies of the three partitioning powers. The end of the Great War brought back Poland's independence. The new Polish Army had many regiments of Uhlans and a Cavalry Training Centre in the town of Grudziądz. It is of this that Rotmistrz Bączkowski writes with such fondness. The soul of a Polish Cavalryman is a unique phenomenon.

This, then, is the background to the tale recounted by Rotmistrz Bączkowski. The rank of 'Rotmistrz', literally 'Master of Squadron' (German and Austrian 'Rittmeister') dates back to the 15th Century when the Polish Rotmistrz would join an army, bringing with him his own Squadron, or 'Rota'. It became officially established in the 19th Century and was then used in independent Poland in the period between the World Wars, being equivalent to the rank of Captain in other formations. In a cavalry setting, so dear to the Polish heart, it has a certain poignant traditional ring and so I have deliberately used the term 'Rotmistrz' in situations which reflect Rotmistrz Tadeusz Bączkowski's close bond with the Cavalry, while generally using the British equivalent rank of 'Captain'.

Foreword

'Rotmistrz', or Captain, Tadeusz Bączkowski was a fairly frequent visitor to the Polish Institute and General Sikorski Museum in London for many years. A quiet, slightly stooped man of few words he would come to visit his younger brother-in-arms from the 9th [Małopolski] Lancers Regiment – Rotmistrz Ryszard Dembiński, then Chairman of the Institute. The two men had in common their work in the Regimental Club and, as it later transpired, also their service in the 1st Polish Armoured Division.

However, whilst Tadeusz Bączkowski frequently recalled his native Brzeżany, Ostróg on the River Horyń, and his service in the 19th [Wołyń] Lancers Regiment, he rarely spoke of his service with the British Forces in West Africa and practically never referred to his service in the 1st Polish Armoured Division. As the proprietor of a printing works, he often printed leaflets, invitations and visiting cards for the Institute. He was seen but rarely heard. He would simply turn up, attend to the various matters which concerned him and leave. Smartly dressed, he was modest and invariably polite. And that is how I continue to remember him.

All the more reason, then, why these short reminiscences which Rotmistrz Bączkowski recorded towards the end of his life should constitute an interesting insight into the life of a man whom I regularly encountered in our Institute, a man devoted to the Polish Cavalry and to the South-Eastern Borderlands which Poland lost after the Second World War.

Krzysztof Barbarski
Chairman,
Polish Institute and General Sikorski Museum,
London, 1 November 2016

Dariusz Szymczyk
travels back in time with
'Rotmistrz' Tadeusz Bączkowski

I arrived in London on 13 September 2012. The aim of my first visit to the British Isles was the Polish Institute and Sikorski Museum, where I intended to carry out research in the archives as part of my doctoral thesis regarding the fate of the soldiers of General Stanisław Maczek's 1st Polish Armoured Division and the paths which led them to the Division. The copious nature of the archives was overwhelming and I decided to extend my stay and to remain in London for some time.

After a few months, Dr Andrzej Suchcitz, Keeper of Archives, noted my interest in the 10th Dragoon Regiment and the histories of its soldiers and he put me in touch with Lieutenant Colonel Zbigniew Makowiecki[1]. During our meeting, Lieutenant Colonel Makowiecki told me about 'Rotmistrz' or Captain Tadeusz Bączkowski, an officer in the 1st Polish Armoured Division, who was now living in the Polish "Kolbe House" retirement home in Ealing Common. I made an appointment and set off for Ealing to interview him. And that, in a nutshell, is how this fascinating adventure began.

The phrase "How I reached the one hundredth milestone", used in the title of the Polish version of this work, refers to Captain Bączkowski's speech during celebrations marking his 100th birthday, to which I was invited. However, before

---

1   Zbigniew Konstanty Bronisław Makowiecki (1917-2017) – born in St. Petersburg (after the 1917 revolution, his family moved to Warsaw). Having completed his officer cadet training, he was assigned to the 1st Light Cavalry Regiment. Immediately before the outbreak of the II World War, he was mobilised and assigned to the 3rd Mounted Rifles Regiment in Wołkowysk. During the first days of September, the Regiment formed part of the Suwałki Cavalry Brigade. Makowiecki fought at Kocko in the final battle of the September 1939 Campaign. He spent the years 1939-1945 as a German POW, and then served in the 10th Dragoon Regiment, a unit of Gen. Stanisław Maczek's 1st Armoured Division. After the war, he settled in London. He was the last Chairman of the Association of Cavalry Regiment Clubs. Lieutenant Colonel Makowiecki was awarded the Polish Cross of Valour, the Knight's Cross of the Polonia Restituta Order, the Gold Cross of Merit, as well as other awards. He lives in London (for more information, see D. Szymczyk, *Zbigniew Makowiecki w obozach jenieckich Wehrmachtu* [Zbigniew Makowiecki in Wehrmacht POW camps], publ. Łambinowicki Rocznik Muzealny 2014, vol. 37, pg. 125–144).

that, there was my first interview with him and then, at the suggestion of my PhD supervisor, Prof. Mieczysław Nurek, a photographic session to illustrate the interview.

Captain Tadeusz Bączkowski was born over one hundred years ago

> ... in a small town called Brzeżany in the Podole Region, located 100 kilometres to the South-East of Lwów. Marshal Rydz-Śmigły was also born and brought up in Brzeżany. [...] I attended High School there. By the time I reached the sixth or seventh class, I had already decided that I wanted to serve in the army. I wasn't interested in any further studies. Most of my friends studied law. In those days, you could live at home in Brzeżany and travel to Lwów for written and oral examinations. Nonetheless, I decided to join the army. The cavalry, to be precise. My experience of horses was confined to my holidays, all of which I spent at my uncle's place in the country where I did what one normally does in the country. I rode out to take part in the haymaking, I brought in the sheaves of corn and rode bareback to water the horses. I spent those first twenty years of my life in a Poland which was more beautiful than it had ever been, even in the times of the Piast and Jagiellonian dynasties. There will never be a Poland like that ever again.[2]

As I came to know those poignant poetic descriptions of life in Poland before the Second World War, I began to immerse myself ever more deeply in the realities of those times.

To me this Rotmistrz, or Captain-of-Horse, became a forebear, a symbol of this land of Poland, an example of how we should strive for complete independence and the freedom which it brings.

> After high school, I enlisted in the army. I spent the first year in the Infantry Officer Cadet Training School. This was a so-called 'unified' course. Before the war, military service was compulsory. On reaching the age of eighteen, everyone was called up. Those who only had a primary education went straight into a regiment. All those who had completed secondary schooling, or matriculation, went to Officer Cadet Training School. The first year, then, was the so-called 'unified' course. Everyone who wanted a military career, whether in the navy, the air-force or the artillery, or in any other field, had to go through it. The

---

2   Excerpt from Dariusz Szymczyk's interview with Captain Tadeusz Bączkowski on 31 July 2013 (referred to herein as: Bączkowski Interview).

assumption was as follows: should an infantryman, an airman or sailor find himself on land and be forced to take part in a battle, or put up a fight in his own defence, he must know how infantrymen fight. Thus, the first year was devoted to infantry training. I spent years two and three in the Cavalry Officer Cadet School in Grudziądz.[3]

On 15 August 1920, on orders issued by the Minister for Military Affairs, a Central Cavalry School was established. This cavalry training centre continued to run in Poland, albeit under various names, to the end of August 1939.

It is hardly surprising that the name "Alma Mater Equitum" became associated with the Cavalry Training Centre in Grudziądz, as its students included: younger age groups intent on a professional military career, reserve warrant officers and most of the older generation of cavalry officers.

Over one thousand officers, and more than three thousand cavalry reserve officer cadets, passed through the Grudziądz military schools, having undergone the required essential training. Some of the latter became officers in the reserves. The number of officers trained in Grudziądz during the interwar period was sufficient for the purposes of mobilisation and secondment to "all the positions in all the cavalry units" in 1939.[4]

Born on 26 October 1913 in Brzeżany, Tadeusz Józef Bączkowski was the son of Jan Bączkowski and Ludwika née Sokołowska. After completing his education in the State High School in Brzeżany, where he passed the final matriculation, or high school leaving examination, in 1933, he commenced the 'unified' course in the Infantry Cadet Officers Training School in Różana on the Narew River. On 11 November, he was promoted to the rank of Lance Corporal Cadet Officer, and on 19 March 1934 to Corporal Cadet Officer. On 15 August 1934, Bączkowski completed training on the 'unified' course and enrolled in the Cavalry Cadet Officer Training School in Grudziądz. Now a Warrant Officer (with seniority as of 19 March 1935), he graduated from the School in Grudziądz on 14 October 1936. Promoted to 2nd Lieutenant with seniority as of 15 October 1936, he was seconded to the 19th Lancers Regiment in Ostróg on the River Horyń as platoon commander in the 2nd Squadron. In September 1937, he was transferred to the position of commander of a cycle platoon. According to the *ordre de bataille* on 23

---

3   *Ibidem.*
4   L. Kukawski, J.S. Tym, *Historia Centrum Wyszkolenia Kawalerii* [The History of the Cavalry Training Centre], in: *Wielka Księga Kawalerii Polskiej 1918–1939. Centrum Wyszkolenia Kawalerii [The Great Book of the Polish Cavalry 1918-1939. The Cavalry Training Centre]*, vol. 47, Warsaw 2013, pg. 8–10.

March 1939, he was seconded to the 19th Lancers Regiment where he continued to fulfil the same function.[5]

At this juncture, it is worth mentioning the history of the 19th Wołyń Lancers Regiment, which was created in September 1920. The units commanded by Major Feliks Jaworski, which constituted its core, were already in existence in July 1917. The re-organised voluntary cavalry brigade, from the ranks of which Major Jaworski selected the best soldiers and the best horses, was reconstituted as the 19th Regiment. Once the individual voluntary cavalry units had arrived in Turów, it took just two months to finalise its reorganisation. On 20 December 1920, the Regiment was given orders to patrol the Polish-Soviet demarcation line. The Regiment remained in Byelorussia [today's Belarus] until March 1922, and in May it was transferred from its location in Głębokie to Ostróg on the River Horyń, where it was garrisoned until 1939. Located just 1.5 kilometres from the border with the USSR, the unit's barracks provided a uniquely atmospheric training ground for the new Regiment.

Until 1938 the Regiment used the name *19. Pułk Ułanów Wołyńskich im. Karola Różyckiego* [19th Wołyń Lancers Regiment, named after Karol Różycki (Commander of the Wołyń Cavalry in 1831)], and was then renamed the 19th Wołyń Lancers Regiment, named after *Edmund* Różycki (Commander of the Uprising in the province of Wołyń in 1863). In Ostróg on 6 August 1924, Marshal Józef Piłsudski presented the 19th Wołyń Lancers Regiment with their colours, funded by the District of Ostróg in recognition of the Regiment's services in the battle for independence.[6]

Until 1939, the Regiment was commanded in turn by: Major Feliks Jaworski (up to June 1921), Lieutenant Colonel Michał Cieński (from 8 August 1921), Colonel Mścisław Butkiewicz (from 10 June 1922), Lieutenant Colonel Zbigniew Brochwicz-Lewiński (from 20 August 1922), Lieutenant Colonel Włodzimierz Kazimierz Bogusz-Roland (from 1 September 1927), Lieutenant Colonel Aleksander Piotraszewski (from March 1929), Lieutenant Colonel Dezyderiusz Zawistowski (from May 1938) and, finally, from 1 February until 29 September 1939, the Regiment was commanded by Lieutenant Colonel Józef Pętkowski.[7]

---

5   R. Rybka, K. Stepan, *Rocznik oficerski 1939. Stan na dzień 23 marca 1939 [Officers' Yearbook 1939. OdB as at 23 March 1939]*, Kraków 2006, pg. 152, 703; Polish Institute and Gen. Sikorski Museum (hereinafter: PISM), A.XII.27/67, Rotmistrz Bączkowski File, Personnel Records for Captain Tadeusz Bączkowski (hereinafter: Service Record File).

6   L. Kukawski, *Historia pułku* [History of the Regiment], in: *Wielka Księga Kawalerii Polskiej 1918– 1939. 19 Pułk Ułanów [The Great Book of the Polish Cavalry 1918-1939. The 19th Lancers Regiment]*, vol. 22, Warsaw 2012, pg. 5–41.

7   *Ibidem*, pg. 76–78.

The 19th Wołyń Lancers Regiment never forgot its founder and first commander, Maj. Feliks Jaworski. Jaworski was a typical wartime commander and life in times of peace most certainly did not suit him – even in the army. He commanded the Regiment until 1921 and was then given an appointment at the Military Academy. He moved from regiment to regiment several times. Feliks Jaworski never married, his greatest love was the army and combat in any form. He was wounded several times but each time the wounds would heal quite quickly. Peacetime 'indolence' did not suit him. He fell ill and was taken to hospital but now the doctors were unable to help him. When war broke out in 1939, he was in Kulparków, near Lwów. In view of the Bolshevik invasion and knowing full well what would happen to him at the hands of the Soviets, the Major's friends attempted to move him to the west of Poland. It is a fact that he never reached Łódź, to which he was being transported. No-one knows what happened to him, he was lost without a trace! Later attempts to find out were unsuccessful.[8]

In 1939, the 19th Wołyń Lancers Regiment was mobilised reasonably quickly and on 19 August, it was transported by train to the station at Radomsko. After disembarkation, it made its way to the area where the Wołyń Cavalry Brigade was concentrated. In the late evening of 31 August, the Regiment carried out an earlier order to prepare to march out and found itself in the Ostrów-Miedźno-Mokra area along with the Wołyń Cavalry Brigade, which formed a part of "Army Group Łódź", covering its left (southern) flank. German units were located according to the new 'Blitzkrieg' doctrine and an attack by the might of the German forces at the point where the Polish "Łódź" and "Kraków" Army Groups met anticipated that the Polish front would be rapidly broken. The Germans planned to reach Warsaw within three days and to force the Polish government to sign a surrender. The Battle of Mokra and Miedźno was one of the biggest and most bloody battles of the September Campaign. Despite the enemy's considerable superiority, its armoured equipment and fire-power, the Wołyń Cavalry Brigade – faced for the first three days of September with the enemy's XVI Panzer Korps commanded by Gen. Erich Hoepner (and especially the 4th Panzer Division, and later units of the 1st Panzer Division) – carried out its task with success, inflicting considerable losses on the enemy.

Already on 1 September, the 19th Lancers Regiment had caused serious

---

8   *Ibidem*, pg. 36–37.

damage to the German invading force. The following day, on the orders of the Brigade Commander, the Regiment drew back. Continously harassed by German air attacks, it fought in the Ostrów and Żeromin districts, and then engaged in a heavy battle at Cytrusowa Wola, where the Wołyń Lancers suffered severe casualties with many dead and wounded. Next, armed with supplies of food and ammunition, the Regiment crossed the River Vistula, and with the Brigade, it joined the ranks of General Władysław Anders's Operational Cavalry Group. On 13 September, a heavy battle was fought for Mińsk Mazowiecki. After the battle, the Regiment began its breakthrough to Rejowce.

The now badly depleted Regiment was assigned to Colonel Jerzy Grobicki's *Kresowa II* collective Cavalry Brigade. When the Germans routed the Brigade during a battle in the Jacnia-Suchowola area during the night of 24 to 25 September, the remainder of the 19th Lancers Regiment tried to break through in the direction of the Hungarian border, all the time being under attack by Soviet units aided by Ukrainians. On 28 September, what was left of the Regiment was taken prisoner by the Red Army and all its officers were murdered by the NKVD.[9]

According to an account by Second Lieutenant Tadeusz Bączkowski, dated 2 January 1940, which can be found in his Records, the mobilisation of the 19th Lancers Regiment took place on 13 August (this is also confirmed by an account given by Captain Antoni Skiba). On its arrival by train at Radomsko station from Ostróg on the River Horyń, the Regiment marched to a location in the Działoszyn district, and on 29 August moved on to Zawada in the Wieluń district. On 30 August, the Regiment halted in a secured location. From 1 to 7 September, Second Lieutenant Bączkowski "took part in combat action". On 8 September, the "Regiment departed" leaving a platoon of cyclists with its commander but without further orders. From 8 to 15 September, the commander and the platoon attempted to reach the following mustering points: Garwolin, Żelechów – Mińsk Mazowiecki, Kałuszyn – Łuków, Radzyń, Włodawa – Osowa. On 13 September, Second Lieutenant Bączkowski formed a platoon in the mustering point in Radzyń and then, on 15 September, a squadron was formed under his command in a mustering point to the south-west of Włodawa. The date of 15 September

---

9   *Ibidem*, pg. 45–61. For more about the 19th Wołyń Lancers Regiment during this period see: A. Skiba, *Boje 19 Pułku Ułanów Wołyńskich w kampanii wrześniowej [The 19th Wołyń Lancers Regiment's battles during the September Campaign]*, London 1971. There, too, you will find more information about Tadeusz Bączkowski dated 1 September, referring to Lieutenant Wojciech Gumiński's 4th Squadron: "At Danków, under threat of being surrounded by tanks and motorcycles, the platoon withdrew after a brief battle. The emplacement was rescued by 2nd Lieut. T. Bączkowski's reconnaissance group, comprising a platoon of cyclists and a platoon of armoured cars" (pg. 30).

also reveals information about the Commander of the Divisional Artillery of the 41st (Reserve) Infantry Division – Colonel Adam Sawczyński, whom the author of the memoirs names as being the officer in command of the mustering point. From 16 to 24 September, Second Lieutenant Bączkowski and his Squadron took part in action with the 41st Infantry Division. On 24 September on the orders of General Piekarski[10] in the village of Lipina, the "squadron was disbanded, arms were destroyed, and the unit began its breakthrough to the Hungarian border". On 9 October, Second Lieutenant Bączkowski crossed the Hungarian border and was interned in a camp for officers in Dömös.[11]

During the first phase, the withdrawal to Hungary took place mainly via the Dukielska and Jabłonowska Passes, and then, once the border had been sealed by the Germans and Ukrainians, mass evacuation stopped and from then on only individuals and small groups managed to cross the no man's land belt.

Initially, escapes from the internment camps were also organised on a mass basis; the escapees did not meet with serious difficulties. The Hungarians were well aware that the Polish Diplomatic Mission in Budapest was responsible for the organisation of these escapes. It was also a known fact that secret institutions in areas of Yugoslavia were also responsible for the success of the evacuations. French and British Diplomatic Missions, too, helped with the organisation of the escapes. "The evacuation procedure was generally well organised, which even officers of the Hungarian *Honvédség, or Homeland Defence, admitted*".[12] Escapees from Hungary headed mainly for Yugoslavia – the comparatively easy border

---

10   Wacław Piekarski (1893–1979) – Major General in the Polish Army. He served in the Polish Legions from 1914 and in the Polish Army when Poland regained independence in 1918. In June 1921, he was a 2nd Lieut. in the 43rd Infantry Regiment. During the period 1922–1924 he studied in the École Supérieure de Guerre in Paris (serving as a superenumerary officer in the 36th Infantry Regiment of the Academic Legion in Warsaw). From January 1925 in Department II (Intelligencee) of the General Staff as Head of Section II. From September 1926 in the General Inspectorate of the Armed Forces as First Officer in the Staff of Lieutenant General Jan Romer, Inspector of the Army. In April 1927, he took command of the 54th Infantry Regiment in Tarnopol. Promoted to Colonel on 1 January 1928. In June 1931 transferred to the Border Defence Corps as Commander of the 4th Brigade of the Border Defence Corps, renamed the "Podole" Frontier Defence Corps Brigade. From October 1935, Deputy Commander of the 11th Carpathian Infantry Division in Stanisławów. From August 1936 to October 1938, Commander of the 29th Infantry Division in Grodno. From October 1938 to August 1939, Head of Department of the Infantry in the Ministry of Military Affairs. Promoted to Major General in March 1939. In the September Campaign, he commanded the 41st Infantry (Reserve) Division, and then the improvised combat group made up of the 33rd Infantry Division and the 41st Infantry Division. Following the defeat, Piekarski was held in a German POW Camp. After the war, he settled in France as an émigré. Director of the Polish Welfare Aid Retirement Home in Lailly-en-Val.
11   PISM, A.XII.27/67, Service Record File.
12   W. Biegański, *Wojsko Polskie we Francji 1939–1940* [The Polish Army in France 1939-1940], Warsaw 1967, pg. 126.

crossing was a result of lack of cooperation between Hungarian and Yugoslavian border guards.

Under pressure from Germany, the Hungarian authorities, though generally well disposed towards the interned Poles, gradually put in motion various military and police directives. In line with a directive issued on 27 October 1939, the police authorities were ordered to arrest potential escapees and to conduct them to the nearest Hungarian guard post. On 21 November, the Hungarian and Yugoslav border defence units signed a cooperation agreement enforcing detainment of Polish nationals attempting to escape from Hungary.[13]

> I escaped from the internment camp and reached Marseilles, via Yugoslavia. At that time, our Consulate in Budapest was still functioning. Colonel Bogoria-Zakrzewski was the Consul at the time and he made it possible for us to reach France with the help of special guides. In Yugoslavia – in Zagreb – we had a guide who piloted us ... We had to wait for some time in the town of Split for a ship. I eventually sailed to France and from then on was in exile in France.[14]

According to details contained in the above-mentioned Personnel Record, and also in a subsequent Record dated 13 March 1946, on 7 December 1939 the Consulate of the Republic of Poland in Budapest issued passport no. 44/1089 to Second Lieutenant Tadeusz Bączkowski. He crossed the no man's land between Hungary and Yugoslavia on 10 December and reported to the Polish Consulate General in Zagreb, and then left for Split. The sea journey to Marseilles lasted from 15 to 19 December. He stayed in the *Camp de Carpiagne* camp near Marseilles from 19 to 27 December. On 29 December, Bączkowski arrived in Paris and reported at the mustering station in Bessières. From 3 January to 4 April 1940, he stayed in the Reserves Training Centre in Sables d'Or and on 5 April was assigned to the 3rd Reconaissance Unit, 3rd Infantry Division, where he took command of a platoon.[15]

The reorganisation of the Polish Army in France dates back to January 1939, when the *Le Nation en temps de Guerre* law came into force. According to the chapter entitled *La Mobilisation*, every foreign citizen enlisting voluntarily in the army during mobilisation would automatically be given French citizenship. This

---

13 *Ibidem*, pg. 122–126.
14 Bączkowski interview. In actual fact, Józef Zarański was Head of the Polish Consulate in Budapest. Under the guise of a Consulate staff member, Colonel Adam Bogoria-Zakrzewski was also in charge of the military evacuation.
15 PISM, A.XII.27/67, Service Record File.

situation aroused the concern of the assistant to the Military Attaché in Paris, Lieutenant Colonel Gustaw Łowczyński, who recalled: "Every Pole enlisting in the French Army would be a loss to Poland. The only means to stop Poles enlisting would be to announce that, in the event of war, Polish Army units would be formed in France."[16]

Details concerning the number of reserve troops in France were obtained from the Ministry of Military Affairs' Manpower Supplementation Department. The proposed formation of Polish units in France was based on this information and sent to Staff Command in Warsaw.

Despite talks between the Polish and French sides in May 1939, as a result of French procrastination, the Franco-Polish Convention dated 19 May 1939, which was to have come into force on signing a political pact (constituting an addendum to the alliance agreed between the two countries in 1921), was not actually signed until 4 September.

Unfortunately, although the Polish Army was being re-formed in France, the project encountered many obstacles on the part of the French. The Poles were not provided with armaments and pressure was put to bear on them to form only infantry units; furthermore, they were warned against attempts to block conscription of Polish nationals who were employed in key areas of French industry.

On 4 January 1940, a new Franco-Polish military pact was signed in Paris which enabled the expansion of the Polish Army. The planned strength of the Polish Army in France was decided on 15 January, during a meeting of the General Staff, led by the Supreme Commander. The envisaged strength was 120,000 troops (40,000 evacuees, 75,000 from France and 5,000 from other countries). By 15 June only 44,500 Poles from France had been mobilised, i.e. 53 percent of the strength of the Polish Army in France (the remaining 47 percent were soldiers evacuated from Hungary, Romania, Lithuania and Latvia). The strength of the Polish Army in France in mid-June 1940 amounted to some 84,500 troops.

Soldiers of the Polish Army fought in the 1940 campaigns not just on French territory but also in Norway where the Independent Podhalański [Highland] Rifle Brigade, with a strength of 4,778 soldiers constituted one third of the total strength of the Allied land forces operating in the area.[17] Of all the Polish units in

---

16 Z. Wawer, E. Pawłowski, Polskie Siły Zbrojne na obczyźnie [Polish Armed Forces in Exile], in: *Wojsko Polskie w II wojnie światowej* [*The Polish Army in the II World War*], ed. E. Pawłowski, Z. Wawer, Warsaw 2005, pg. 151.

17 *Ibidem*, pg. 151–154.

France it was this splendid Brigade which suffered the most tragic consequences, its potential being shamefully wasted. As a result of an inaccurate assessment of the Brigade, which stopped off in Great Britain on its return journey from Norway, it was directed to France, to the defence of Brittany. In view of the armistice, on 17 June 1940, General Antoine Béthouart gave permission to its commander, General Zygmunt Bohusz-Szyszko, for evacuation to England, with the reservation that all those troops with ties in France were to remain in France. Only a few hundred troops managed to make it to Great Britain.

The 3rd Infantry Division, together with the 3rd Reconnaissance Unit, in which Tadeusz Bączkowski served in France in 1940, suffered a similar tragic fate. With a strength of some 9,600 troops it was involved in the defence of Brittany. When it transpired that the French had no intention of defending Brittany, the Commander of the Division, Colonel Tadeusz Zieleniewski decided to withdraw behind the River Loire. Then, in view of the impossibility of crossing the river in the Saint-Nazaire area, and the stringent orders of the commander of the defence of Brittany, General René Altmayer, that the Polish Division should surrender to the Germans, Colonel Zieleniewski took the decision to disband the Division.

The problems facing the Polish Commander did not end there. On 19 June 1940, Colonel Zieleniewski reported the disbanding of his Division to General Louis Faury who was preparing for the evacuation. In return he was ordered to: "Gather your Division together again and report to the Germans."[18] The Polish commander did not carry out this order. Having arrived in Vannes, he reported to General Bleu on 20 June and asked for transport facilities for the Division. Once more he met with disappointment. The French general declared that he did not have any transport means available and, anyway, Polish troops were not allowed to embark for England – they were to remain as a consolidated unit and to await the arrival of the Germans. He also threatened to arrest all those who disobeyed the order.

When the Division was disbanded, those of the Polish soldiers who lived in France returned to their homes and the remainder, in small groups and in entire units, made for the ports. Eventually, some 2,500 soldiers were evacuated to Great Britain from the ports in Le Croisic, La Turballe, Quibéron and from the islands of Belle-Île and Île d'Yeu.[19]

A group belonging to the 3rd Reconnaissance Unit, to which Second Lieutenant Bączkowski belonged, reached the port in St. Nazaire independently

---

18 *Ibidem*, pg. 161.
19 *Ibidem*, pg. 160–164.

and was evacuated from there to England. After the Fall of France, General Władysław Sikorski once again set about re-forming the Polish Armed Forces. In accordance with the Polish-British Pact of 19 June 1940, the Polish Army was to be re-formed in the British Isles. As a result of an order issued by the Supreme Commander and dated 5 July 1940, work began on the organisation of the 1st and 2nd Rifle Brigades. The 3rd Rifle Brigade came into being on the strength of an order dated 23 August.[20]

Second Lieutenant Tadeusz Bączkowski arrived at Falmouth in the British Isles on 23 June 1940. He was assigned to the reconnaissance unit of the 1st Rifle Brigade and took command of a platoon. On 10 December, he was transferred to an equivalent unit in the 7th Cadre Rifle Brigade[21], established in accordance with an order dated 21 June 1940. Initially it was stationed in the Dunfermline area of Scotland as a reserve unit for the I Corps, to strengthen the defence of Donibristle and the port of Rosyth. In March 1941, it took command of the defence of the Brechin-Montrose-Edzell coastline. That month, too, the King and Queen took the salute of a march past by the Polish unit in Forfar.[22]

A detailed assessment and opinion given on 7 February 1941 by his first superior (for 1940), the Commander of the 7th Reconnaissance Unit, the 7th Cadre Rifle Brigade, Cavalry Lieutenant Colonel Bronisław Mokrzycki, provides a valuable source of information about Second Lieutenant Tadeusz Bączkowski: "Manly character, stubborn, reserved. Morale above reproach. Fairly narrow range of intelligence and interests. V[ery] physically fit although externally gives the impression of being somewhat uncared for. His knowledge of the skills required of a platoon leader are adequate. This officer came to us with a very negative assessment which he affirms. He requires caring and friendly support. He may improve and a turn for the better is already noticeable. In 1939, he was said to be a v[ery] good unit com[mander] in the field (according to accounts given by officers). (...) He has grounded his knowledge and reviewed it but, above all, he has acquired the necessary confidence in himself (...). He has the makings of a good officer and platoom commander in action, and a good instructor."[23]

On 20 March 1941, Second Lieutenant Bączkowski was promoted to the rank of Lieutenant. From 8 September 1941 to 7 October 1943 he served with British Army formations in the colonies.[24]

---

20 *Ibidem*, pg. 168–171.
21 PISM, A.XII.27/67, Service Record File, References for 1940 (Officers' Service Records).
22 *Piechota 1939–1945* [Infantry, 1939-1945] 1972, file. 9/10, pg. 93.
23 PISM, A.XII.27/67, Service Record File, References for 1940 (Officers' Service Records).
24 *Ibidem*, Service Record File (British order no. NO: P/204604/).

In the spring of 1941, rumours began to circulate which indicated a desire to resolve the problem of an excessive number of Polish officers in Scotland at that time. There was talk of jobs in the armaments industry and a plan to establish various combat units composed solely of officers. Hearsay claimed that the Belgians had applied to Gen. Sikorski for permission to employ five hundred Polish officers.

In the summer of 1941, news spread about a plan for voluntary conscription for service in the British colonies in West Africa. The British were willing to take on four hundred Polish officers. Applicants had to go through a verification procedure – only young, healthy and strong officers were accepted. The draft board, which included a variety of medical specialists, non-commissioned officers and clerks from the British Medical Corps, selected the healthiest candidates.[25] The Polish Supreme Command gave its consent for just three hundred officers to leave.

Of the almost eight hundred Polish officers who applied to leave for West Africa, a total of only 273 officers served in Africa for periods of varying length. The Polish officers served in Nigeria, on the Gold Coast, in Sierra Leone and the Gambia. "The Supreme Commander, General Sikorski, saw off the departing officers with Order No. 9 dated 3 September 1941, in which he assured them that this service would be treated as active wartime military service in the Polish Army, and stressed that they continue to serve their Country."[26]

Departure was divided into three stages. The first, consisting of over one hundred officers, reached Africa on 13 October 1941, the second took place in November of the same year, while the third contingent did not leave until the end of December. Additionally, some officers made their way to Africa individually and a small group of doctors did not arrive until June 1942.[27] Lieutenant Bączkowski reached Sierra Leone with the third contingent and was assigned to an Infantry Regiment. He figures on the list for 1 January 1942. He served with the British rank of lieutenant.[28]

Having completed his two-year contract, Lieutenant Bączkowski returned to Great Britain and, on 8 October 1943, was seconded to the Infantry Training

---

25 E. Eckert, *Eksperyment. Polscy oficerowie w Afryce Zachodniej w latach 1941–1943* [An experiment. Polish Officers in West Africa in the period 1941-1943], *PISM. Materiały – Dokumenty – Źródła – Archiwalia"* [PISM. Materials – Documents – Sources – Archives] 1988, file. 4, pg. 1–4.

26 PISM, A.XII.17/1, Col. Włodzimierz Ludwig, *Szkic historyczny tyczący się pobytu oficerów polskich w Afryce Zachodniej* [Short History of the Polish Officers stationed in West Africa], Achimota, 28 May 1943.

27 *Ibidem.*

28 PISM, A.XII.17/2, *Wykaz oficerów polskich w Afryce Zachodniej* [List of Polish Officers in West Africa].

Centre Supply Battalion as second-in-command of a company. By 14 October he had already been transferred to the Infantry Training Centre (Supply Battalion), and then on 2 November to the Central Regulations Commission in the role of Interpreter. On 24 January 1944, he was transferred to Staff Command of the 1st Armoured Division, commanded by General Stanisław Maczek, as Liaison Officer.[29]

I arrived at the place where the Staff of the 1st [Armoured] Division was stationed[30] – in Peebles, in the south-east of Scotland [...] to receive my assignment. I reported to the Chief-of-Staff[31], Colonel Stankiewicz[32] [...]. He decided that, since I knew English, I should stay there as a liaison officer. I was one of three liaison officers. One was attached to the Rifle Brigade – the Infantry. One to 'the English', and I to the 10th Brigade. There were three of us: Gilewicz[33], Fudakowski[34] and me. Each day I would travel to the regiments of

29 PISM, A.XII.27/67, Service Record File.
30 "It was not until February 1940 when the threat of invasion had passed that it became possible to obtain the agreement of the English authorities. On 25 February 1942, the first order of the Supreme Commander was issued, ordering the formation of an armoured division" (*1. Dywizja Pancerna w walce. Praca zbiorowa*, [1st Armoured Division in battle. Collective Work] Brussels 1947, reprint: Bielsko-Biała [2002], pg. 18).
31 Ludwik Stankiewicz became Chief-of-Staff of the 1st Armoured Division, replacing Col. Jerzy Levittoux (who was killed the previous day) on 19 July 1944, therefore, during the period to which the author refers, he was not yet Chief-of-Staff but an operational officer (Head of Command Unit III) of the 1st Armoured Division.
32 Ludwik Antoni Stankiewicz (1908–1956) – Lieutenant in Regular Infantry Officer Corps. According to records as at 23 March 1939, student at the Warsaw Staff Academy [*Wyższa Szkoła Wojenna w Warszawie*] (1937–1939). According to *ordre de bataille* records of the 10th Armoured Cavalry Division on 1 September 1939, armoured forces Captain (Aide in HQ). After evacuation to Hungary, he managed to break through to France, via Yugoslavia. Took part in the defence of France as operational officer in the 10th Armoured Cavalry Brigade. When the Brigade was disbanded, he made his way through France, Spain and Portugal and arrived in Liverpool, GB. Promoted to the rank of Major in January 1943. Working closely with Gen. Stanisław Maczek, he took part in the entire combat trail of the 1st Armoured Division – from Falaise to Wilhelmshaven. In recognition of remarkable service in the battles of Normandy (particularly in the Chambois region) he was promoted to the rank of Lieutenant Colonel. Retired from active service on 30 June 1950 and settled in London. Worked in the V. and F. Monaco Motors Company and participated actively in the life of the émigré community. Awarded, among others, the Order of Virtuti Military V Class, the Cross of Valour twice, the Gold Cross with Swords, and various foreign decorations. He died in London and was buried in Brompton Cemetery.
33 Probably Jerzy Gilewicz (1915–2014) – 1st Armoured Division cadre from 7 November 1943. Transferred to Armoured Grenadier Division on 24 November 1944.
34 Zygmunt Jan Fudakowski (1915–2000) – 2nd Lieutenant (Reserves) in the Cavalry Officer Corps. From 5 August 1944 to 10 April 1945, liaison officer in the 1st Armoured Division (PISM, A.XII.27/67, Z. Fudakowski's Service Record File). Former Adjutant to Gen. Władysław Sikorski, decorated with the Polonia Restituta Order – V Class, the Republic of Poland's Order of Merit IV Class, the Cross of Valour, the Gold Cross of Merit with Swords, as well as other Polish, British and French awards. He died in Johannesburg (for more information, see: *Zygmunt Fudakowski*, [in:] *Rycerze, Infułat i Pastor,*

the 10th Brigade, either with orders from the Division Commander for them, or with their reports – no matter whether by day or night.[35]

On 9 September 1944. Lieutenant Bączkowski was promoted to the rank of *Rotmistrz* [Captain]. On 23 September, he was transferred to the Infantry Training Centre and Reserves Centre of the 1st Armoured Division. Under the heading '2 January 1945', we find information concerning the return of Captain Bączkowski to the 1st Armoured Division (as liaison officer).[36]

From September 1939 to the end of April 1945, the 10th Motorised Cavalry Brigade, the 10th Armoured Cavalry Brigade and then the 1st Armoured Division, commanded by General Stanisław Maczek, fought some 50 battles and skirmishes, enduring three major campaigns of the 2nd World War (Poland 1939, France 1940 and 1944). Its campaign trail led the 1st Armoured Division via France, Belgium and Holland to Germany and there – in the largest German military port of Wilmhelmshaven – it raised the red and white Polish flag.[37]

Unfortunately, however, despite the enormous sacrifice and suffering, despite the heavy losses sustained in combat, the soldiers of the 1st Armoured Division – like most of those serving in the Polish Armed Forces in the West – were not able to celebrate the victory and their return to their native Poland proved problematical.

According to data as at December 1945, there were approximately 250,000 troops serving in the ranks of the Polish Armed Forces in the West [PSZ], under British operational command. Many of them had found their way into the ranks of the PSZ as German Army POWs, some had been forcibly conscripted as slave labour by the German Todt Organisation, while others had endured the Polish Army's long trail through the USSR, the Middle East and Italy. Among them, too, were those who had been evacuated from France in 1940, as well as officers and men from German POW camps.[38]

Poland had lost its sovereignty and its government was now subordinate to

---

czyli wojenne wspomnienia spod Krzyża Południa [Knights, Monsignor and Pastor, or Wartime Memoirs from beneath the Southern Cross], ed. A. Krzychylkiewicz, A. Romanowicz, Warsaw 2013, pg. 13–129).

35 Bączkowski interview.

36 "Throughout his work in the capacity of Liaison Officer he carried out all tasks with great devotion and without regard for his own safety" (PISM, A.XII.85/117/4, Personnel Journal, Application by Lt. Col. Ludwik Stankiewicz to award Capt. Tadeusz Bączkowski the Silver Cross of Valour with Swords, supported in his own handwriting by Gen. Stanisław Maczek, Commander of the 1st Armoured Division).

37 *Żołnierze Generała Maczka [General Maczek's Soldiers]*, ed. Z. Mieczkowski, together with S. Wyganowski and W. Żakowski, Warsaw-London 2003, pg. 30.

38 For more information, see: J. Zubrzycki, *Polish Immigrants in Britain*, The Hague 1956, pg. 57.

Stalin. Polish soldiers, like all other Poles who were currently away from Poland, now faced a choice between exile and a return to their homeland. Choosing to wait for more propitious times for Poland, approximately half a million Poles chose life in exile. These people were staunch patriots and they treated their choice as an expression of their protest against the political situation which had been forced on Poland. Their mission was to strive for the liberation of Poland. The political institutions, community organisations, ex-combatant and cultural associations which they established provided an alternative, a rebellion against the totalitarian system which had taken over Poland. The stance and the actions of these people who epitomised the ideals of an independent Republic of Poland led to a situation in which the Soviet enforced authorities in Poland considered them to be the sole organised anti-Communist community – until such time as a democratic opposition was established in Poland.[39]

When military operations ceased, Captain Bączkowski remained in the ranks of the 1st Armoured Division which, as part of the British sector, occupied the north-western territories of Germany. On 8 February 1946, he was transferred to the Reserves Centre of the 1st Armoured Division and reported there on 13 February. From 14 May, he served in the Services Training Centre, simultaneously holding a secondment to the Command of the I Corps's Materials Depot. Next, from 14 August to 31 December 1946, he was temporarily assigned to the Port Liaison Section in Dover (extended to 31 March 1947).[40]

On 5 April 1947, Captain Bączkowski signed up with the Polish Resettlement Corps [PKPR][41], where he remained until 4 April 1949, when he was finally discharged and became a civilian.[42] He settled in London and throughout this long period of exile, managed to cope very well. For almost fifty years, he ran his own printing firm – the *Omega Press*. When he retired, he devoted his time to the community, working with organisations which cultivated and perpetuated Poland's military traditions. He returned to Poland for the first time in 1989 and from then on would regularly visit his beloved Homeland.

As I have already mentioned, I met Captain Bączkowski thanks to his friend, Lieutenant Colonel Zbigniew Makowiecki. During our first meeting, which took

39 A. Friszke, *Życie polityczne emigracji [Political life in exile]*, Warsaw 1999, pg. 5–6.
40 PISM, A.XII.27/67, Service Record File.
41 For more about the Polish Resettlement Corps, see M. Nurek, *Gorycz zwycięstwa. Los Polskich Sił Zbrojnych na Zachodzie po II wojnie światowej 1945–1949 [The Bitterness of Victory. The Fate of the Polish Armed Forces in the West after WW2, 1945-1949]*, Gdańsk 2009; J.A. Radomski, *Demobilizacja Polskich Sił Zbrojnych na Zachodzie w latach 1945–1951 [The Demobilisation of the Polish Armed Forces in the West during the period 1945-1951]*, Kraków 2009.
42 PISM, A.XII.27/67, Service Record File.

place on 31 July 2013, the Captain expressed his pleasure in the fact that I was studying for a doctorate and that I had specifically chosen the fate of the soldiers of Gen. Maczek's 1st Armoured Division to be the subject of my thesis. Even after that first encounter, I was still not aware of how lucky I was. After some time – and again thanks to Lieutenant Colonel Makowiecki – I took part in a celebration of Captain Bączkowski's 100th birthday. Later, I received extracts from his memoirs, which were being transcribed by Julita Prabucka and Danuta Wencel. There began a series of Sunday meetings with living Polish history; apart from Captain Bączkowski and myself, Danuta Wencel also took part in these sessions.

Together, we experienced many unforgettable moments. As a PhD student in the Department of History, History of Art and Archeology of the University of Gdańsk, I was afforded the great privilege of working on these memoirs. This honour will stay with me all my life.

Rotmistrz Tadeusz Bączkowski died on 21 January 2015 in London. The funeral Mass took place on 30 January in London's Polish Church of St. Andrzej Bobola. On 7 March, accompanied by a Polish Army Guard of Honour, his ashes were laid to rest in his wife's family tomb in Podkowa Leśna, on the outskirts of Warsaw.

A great patriot, a man of honour, a knight of the Republic of Poland, awarded the Knight's Cross of the Polonia Restituta Order, the Cross of Valour,[43] the Silver Cross of Merit with Swords, the War Medal, as well as British and French medals. He passed away to his Eternal Watch, leaving behind an untarnished memory and the love of his fellow Man.

Dariusz Szymczyk
London, April 2015

---

43 PISM, R 1391, doc. 76, Directive of the President of the Republic of Poland dated 30 December 1949, regarding award of the Cross of Valour for courage and gallantry in the September Campaign of 1939 to the following soldiers: No. 46. 2nd Lieut. Bączkowski [Tadeusz] Cycle Platoon, 19th Lancers Regiment, KW 1 [Cross of Valour for the first time] (signed by President August Zaleski and the Minister of Military Affairs, Gen. Roman Odzieżyński).

1

1913–1933: Schooldays

I was born on 26 October 1913 in Brzeżany. A mistake occurred in émigré documents, giving the date as 28 October which subsequently stuck. Brzeżany is a small town in the Tarnopol province, lying on the Lwów-Podhajce rail route, with some 15,000 inhabitants. Located in a beautiful part of Podole, it stands on picturesque, hilly and wooded terrain. In those days, the greatest attraction of Brzeżany was a large lake – one kilometre wide and three kilometres in length – and the splendid, enormous castle belonging to the Sieniawski family.

The castle sustained damage during the First World War but survived to the Second World War and was used by the Army as a materials depot. It contained several apartments, allotted to military families. The castle was [once] very magnificent, with richly furnished interiors, and was often referred to as the 'Louvre of the East'. It was visited by illustrious European families (I had a postcard showing Tsar Paul's visit to the Sieniawski family[1]). Near the castle was a chapel with splendid sculptures, statues and marble family tombs. The chapel was still in use up to the Second World War and the Army would attend Holy Mass there. After WW2, the chapel sustained barbaric damage – all the statues were smashed, the sculptures and marble sarcophagi destroyed. With time, the entire area of the castle and its surrounds fell into ruin and decay.

Apart from its Polish inhabitants, a large number of Armenians, Czechs, Ruthenians and Jews lived in Brzeżany. Despite their different backgrounds, all these groups lived together in perfect harmony. There were no ethnic or national divides (I know of no instance of anti-semitism).

Apart from the castle in Brzeżany, there was also a splendid Catholic parish church, which served as the garrison church. In addition, there was an Armenian church – that, too, was richly appointed. The town also boasted a magnificent Orthodox church.

In the town centre, the Market Square was enhanced by the square edifice of the Town Hall. It was there that a high school was located – roughly until the

---

1   Probably a mistake. The Sieniawski family could have been visited by Tsar Peter the Great, godfather to Maria Zofia Sieniawska. No Tsar named Paul could have visited the Sieniawski family in its family seat because Sieniawa was taken over by the Czartoryski family in approximately 1731. (note: A.Ś.-J.).

1920s. It was later moved to a new, purpose-built building.

Immensely popular was the "Sokół"[2] Gymnastics Society [a clandestine paramilitary organisation – Trans.], which drew many members – mostly young people (my youngest brother, Władysław, was a member). The Society was based in a building with the sculpture of a falcon on the façade. Theatrical performances and other events were organised there. Nearby was a sports field, where sporting competitions and gymnastics events took place.

Also popular among the young people was the *Sieniawa* Sports Club. Football was not favoured by the school staff and, during the initial period, those pupils who took part in the sport did so discreetly; attitudes later changed, however. I remember part of a song on the subject:

> Axe and hoe, footyball
> Not allowed on the field
> Not on Sieniawa's field
> If Gronik [trainer] spots you
> He'll have your guts for garters

In addition to our high school, there were two 7-class primary schools (one for boys and one for girls) and a girls' teacher training college. Boys from the local villages were boarders and had living quarters and full board. The boarding school was run by Father Marcinkiewicz, the scripture teacher. The priest encouraged the high school pupils to do the cleaning and to tend the gardens; in return he allowed them to listen to the wireless. Those were the early days of the crystal radio receiver. The pupils would sit on a bench, the priest would hold one headphone to the ear of the first pupil and the other to the next boy's ear; the boys crowded together while the priest operated the tuning knob, searching for the radio signal.

We had a good team of teachers in our high school and the level of teaching and lessons was very good. I, myself, did not have any difficulty with learning. In hindsight, however, I do regret that we only learned early Polish history, starting

---

2   The Polish *Sokół* [Falcon] Gymnastics Society promoted fitness and sport, as well as pro-independence traditional moral values and was set up in Lwów in 1867. From 1885, it was also active in the Prussian partition, and from 1905 as an illegal organisation in the Russian governed Kingdom of Poland. In 1919, the Polish Gymnastics Societies from under the three partitions of Poland merged into a single organisation with headquarters in Warsaw. The *Sokół* Society continued to exist until September 1939. Its activities were later renewed in 1989 (*Nowa Encyklopedia Powszechna PWN [The PWN New General Encyclopaedia]*, editor-in-chief: D. Kalisiewicz, vol. 5: *P–S*, Warsaw 1997, pg. 932).

with Mieszko I – the first Polish king – to modern times, rather than from the creation of the Legions [during World War I] to earlier history. I am annoyed that our history teacher never took us to the Sieniawski castle, for instance, which means I never saw the richly decorated chapel, the splendid marbles, sculptures, statues and sarcophagi, all of which survived until the Second World War (with minor damage). It was the subsequent German occupation, followed by the Soviet occupation and the period of the Polish People's Republic [PRL][3], which led to the almost complete destruction of the castle and the total devastation of the chapel.

In the high-school we had a male choir led by the headmaster, Mr Rajter – later shot by the Germans in Ruryski. Apart from the choir, the school ran other clubs for the young people – such as scouting, a philatelic society etc. Among my school-friends there were many amateur actors, writers and directors. They were all members of the drama club, which produced events and patriotic shows. These took place in the *Sokół* building, which was the best venue for such events. The revue which was produced once a year was a particularly popular event. The concept, script and direction was entirely the work of our colleagues in the club. I remember a few extracts from one of these revues in which the choir, the dance club and the orchestra took part.

> ... Brzeżany
> When you see this town from afar
> Your heart will jump with joy
> You'll dream of it
> You'll think of it
> And love it
> Everyone knows Brzeżany
> ... Brzeżany – wondrous, beloved town
> Everyone knows everyone else
> They'll gossip about you
> And have fun with you.

At first, this song was sung at the opening of the revue by a choir hidden behind the curtain and accompanied by the orchestra. At the words "have fun with you", the curtain would rise revealing the choir and a group of dancers at the

---

3   Brzeżany was never incorporated in the borders of the Polish People's Republic.

back of the stage. White petticoats and colourful skirts twirled to the tempo of a lively *kujawiak* dance. The delighted audience stood and clapped.

I remember another extract from a text sung by my older brother, Kazimierz. He wore a wide-brimmed Spanish hat, dark glasses and a long cloak:

> A young calf frisks in the meadow
> Fleas jump around on the bed
> As my heart leaps with you
> I sing my praises
> For my Marzenna
> Peek from your balcony, Madonna, peek.

I remember another sketch, too. Two newsboys are reading the ads. One of them reads out the beginning of an ad (a young lass seeking a husband), the second reads out the end of another ad (about a sofa for sale). The end result was an amusing announcement:

> I. Lass seeks marriage.
> II. Sofa for sale.
> I. Pretty lass eager for a husband.
> II. Legs still strong, little used.

Until 1918, Brzeżany was part of the Austrian partition of Poland. The 10th Regiment of Dragoons was stationed here. I had a postcard entitled *The Year 1917*. It pictured the mobilised regiment in extended line formation in the market square between the Orthodox Church and the Town Hall. I am sure the entire town of Brzeżany observed the scene – including me. I was four years old at the time. It was quite likely the day when the regiment rode out of Brzeżany.

Platoon Leader Tomasz Rydz served in the 10th Dragoon Regiment. He was the father of the future Marshal of Poland, Edward Rydz-Śmigły, who was born and educated in Brzeżany and was one of the first to join the [Polish] Legions.

The death of my mother, Ludwika née Sokołowska, marred my early childhood. I remember the terrible feeling of emptiness which overwhelmed our family, and how sad my siblings (I had three brothers and one sister)[4] were after her death.

---

4 Sister, Maria, the youngest sibling, author's elder brother, Kazimierz, younger brother Jan and Władysław, the youngest of the brothers.

My memories of my first years in school are generally positive. I remember the large, modern school building and the team of older, experienced teachers who were strict but just. Among my school colleagues were some who were special friends. In many cases, friendships forged in the classroom lasted throughout the years I spent in Poland and later continued in exile.

Summer holidays are something which I remember and which I recall with pleasure. Somehow, the weather seemed different in those days. I spent the warm, sunny days with my friends on the lake. Nearby was a vegetable farm belonging to the parents of one of them and we were allowed to visit the tomato plantation when we were thirsty. An even greater holiday attraction, however, was when my brothers and I went to visit our uncle in the country.

My grandfather, whom I never met, must have been a wealthy man (the roof of our house in the country had a metal roof while all the other houses in the village of Rohaczyn only had thatched roofs). My grandfather divided his estate between his two sons. He passed the farm on to the elder son and sent my father off to gain an education – so we had the best of both worlds. Rohaczyn in the Brzeżany district was inhabited by Poles and Ruthenians, who lived together in perfect harmony and mixed marriages were a frequent occurence. Nationalist attitudes were first aroused by the Austrians and then by Russian [!] students studying at Polish universities.

In those childhood days, we were interested in everything: the farm and the animals, the meadow where we could run barefoot on the dewy grass, and the stream which flowed nearby – they all held secrets which we were keen to discover.

It was then, too, that I met and fell forever in love with horses. I was to prove this many years later when I funded the *Medzio* challenge prize, thus honouring Major Feliks Jaworski's horse. Medzio continued to live [in Ostróg] in grace and favour in the 19th [Lancers] Regiment until September 1939.

It would, nonetheless, be untrue for me to say that I was then already dreaming of a sabre in my hand, a chestnut mount, the Cavalry Training School in Grudziądz and of Honorary Rotmistrz Karola[5] – no, the decision to devote

---

5   Karola Skowrońska (born 1944) – librarian, cultural and community worker involved with Grudziądz. Co-founder and first Chairman (1976–2007) of the Grudziądz Cultural Association. Since 1991, she has chaired the Foundation for the Preservation of the Polish Cavalry Tradition, which perpetuates the traditions of the pre-war Cavalry Training Centre and it was she who initiated the annual Gatherings of Cavalrymen of the II Polish Republic, in Grudziądz. She presented a proposal to set up a series of exhibition halls in the Museum in Grudziądz in 1994, devoted to the Traditions of the Polish Cavalry. An honorary member of nine Cavalry Regiments of the II Republic of Poland, she is the only woman to hold the rank of Honorary *Rotmistrz*, or Captain-of-Horse. Member of the Committee for the rebuilding of the 'Polish Soldier's Monument', the construction of the Katyń Memorial and

myself to professional military service, and the cavalry in particular, came much later – at a time when one begins to give thought to the choice of a future career. Two older colleagues helped me in making up my mind: Zbyszek Bojanowski[6], graduate of the Grudziądz Cavalry Training Centre in 1934, and Zbyszek Malawski[7] (1935). I had long discussions with them about the traditions of the Grudziądz Cavalry Training Centre and the sight of them on parade bearing their sabres and wearing their long coats and amaranth-coloured cap-bands reinforced my resolve.

Therefore, when – in accordance with the law and regulations – the time was ripe, I applied to the [Regional] Reserves Command which directed eighteen-year olds to relevant schools.

---

the Monument of a Lancer with a young girl; she initiated the unveiling of many memorial plaques in Grudziądz. Skowrońska received several state and professional awards. More about her in the Epilogue (note: A.Ś.-J.).

6   Zbigniew Jan Bojanowski (1912–1987) – graduated from the Grudziądz Cavalry Officers Training School with the rank of 2nd Lieutenant; on 19 March 1938 promoted to the rank of Lieutenant in the Regular Cavalry Officers' Corps. According to OdB as at 23 March 1939, seconded to the 6th Lancers Regiment as Platoon Commander. According to personnel records as at 2 December 1942, with the rank of Captain, Second-in-Command of Command Squadron of the Motorised Rifle Battalion (one of the rifle battalions in the 1st Armoured Division prior to its re-organisation, and re-grouped from the Reconnaissance Unit of the 10th Armoured Cavalry Brigade and from part of the disbanded Heavy Machine Gun Battalion) on an order issued by the Supreme Commander on 26 February 1942. According to the Membership Record of the 10th Dragoon Regiment Unit Association, his last three positions in the Polish Armed Forces during the period 1939–1946 were: Second-in-Command of a Squadron of the 10th Dragoon Regiment, Squadron Commander in the same Regiment and Acting Second-in-Command to the Commander of the 24th Lancers Regiment. From 1946, held the rank of Major in the Cavalry. The end of the war found him in Great Britain where he trained as a confectioner. A member of Branch 11 of the Association of Polish Ex-Combatants. Died in London. His ashes were interred in his family grave in Warsaw's Powązki Cemetery.

7   Zbigniew Hipolit Malawski (1912–1939) – graduated from the Grudziądz Cavalry Officers Training School with the rank of 2nd Lieutenant in 1935; then promoted to the rank of Lieutenant in the Cavalry Regular Officers' Corps in 1939. According to OdB as at 23 March 1939, assigned for service with the 26th Lancers Regiment as Platoon Commander. In September 1939, regular service Lieutenant of Cavalry – Commander of 1st Heavy Machine Gun Squadron in 26th Lancers Regiment. Killed in action on 30 September in the Hussaków area.

2

1933–1934: Różan on the River Narew

Officer Cadet School

Until recently, military service in Poland was compulsory. On reaching the age of eighteen, young men were obliged to apply to the Regional Reserves Unit [PKU] which, after examining them carefully, sent boys with a lower educational level to relevant military units, and those who had completed high school and passed their matriculation examinations to relevant reserve officer cadet schools. Those who wanted to pursue a professional military career were directed by the PKU to the Infantry Officer Cadet School, the first year of which was based in Różana on the River Narew.

When the time came, I stood before the Brzeżany PKU commission and having successfully passed the tests, I was referred to Różan on the River Narew.

In Różan we were divided into three companies: 9th, 10th and 11th. Each of them consisted of three platoons. I was assigned to the 2nd Platoon, 10th Company. The Company Commander was Captain Marcinkiewicz[8], and my Platoon Commander [Lieut.] Rozborski[9]. The Sergeant, Company Sergeant Major and non-commissioned officers taught us everything a soldier needs to know.

Each company was quartered in a separate building and had its own kitchen. The Company Sergeant Major was responsible for supplies, he ran the morning roll-call and reported to the Company Commander. Each of us was given military

---

8 Stefan Marcinkiewicz (born 1896) – Captain of infantry from 1923. In 1932, seconded to the Infantry Officer Cadet Training School in Ostrów Mazowiecki. Awarded the Cross of Valour three times, and the Silver Cross of Merit.

9 Antoni Rozborski (1900–1961) – infantry Lieutenant from 1925. In 1932, assigned to service in the Infantry Officer Cadet Training School in Ostrów Mazowiecki. Holder of the Cross of Valour (four times for the Polish-Bolshevik War and once for the Second World War). According to OdB as at 23 March 1939, Commander of 2nd Company, the 5th Podhalański [Highland] Rifles Regiment. On 21 September 1939, together with the remnants of the Regiment and other units, crossed the border to Hungary. In France until 1940 as deputy commander of the II Battalion, the 4th Warsaw Infantry Rifles Regiment, part of the 2nd Infantry Rifles Division. Died in hospital in London, interred in New Chiswick Cemetery.

equipment and weapons while our personal equipment included a bed, cupboard, stool, uniform, boots etc.

Lectures on military and social subjects were given by officer-lecturers, following an established curriculum. Non-commissioned officers ran classes in subjects such as gymnastics and drill, weapons, their use and maintenance, and marksmanship. They taught us discipline and orderliness; in the case of the latter, we were subjected to various inspections. I vividly recall inspection of cupboards in my platoon, when we stood beside our open cupboards and the Sergeant checked their tidiness. When he noticed a mess in my neighbour's cupboard, he commented with typical military directness: "Looks like the inside of a whorehouse". My colleague preferred to agree with the Sergeant rather than argue with him and answered: "Yes, Sir, but at least it's an artistic whorehouse". "Don't give me lip, boy, jump to it and tidy it up," the Sergeant ordered. My colleague wanted to butter the sergeant up and to avoid further repercussions, and added: "Sergeant, Sir, rumour has it that you're about to be promoted." Feigning anger but obviously pleased, the Sergeant replied: "Just let me catch that there 'Rumour' and I'll have his guts for garters!"

Sometimes, the Sergeant or one of the non-coms would play a trick on us. I remember once at morning roll-call the Sergeant asked: "Which of the officer cadets would like to be excused from today's afternoon classes and write letters instead?" Naturally, a whole forest of hands shot up. "Report outside the building at 2 o'clock," the Sergeant ordered. At two o'clock he led the troop of 'writers', armed with their writing materials, to the mess room where, instead of writing letters, they had to scrub the tables and benches.

And so, amid constant activity and bustle, the end of the academic year drew nearer – along with that dreaded final examination, on which everything depended. My entire future! And what happens if I don't get into Grudziądz? I certainly did not have a proverbial 'aunty' in the Ministry of Military Affairs, nor any other influential contacts. The situation was very difficult. For every one-hundred applicants, there were only thirty places assigned to Różan. The same examination result as mine, or an even better one, could be achieved by many of my colleagues who were intent on getting into Grudziądz. It was no good counting on a stroke of luck. I did, however, count on the support of my guardian, St. Jude the Apostle, whom I regularly 'bribed' by dropping a coin in the collecting box of this patron saint for desperate cases. Deep inside, though, I counted on the help of someone very dear to me, someone who was in heaven and who watched over me and took care of me. I hoped that this guardian spirit would whisper in the ears of the person placing a tick against the names of hopeful applicants and that, thanks to her, a tick would also be placed against my name. Imagine my relief and joy when I did, indeed, see that √ tick by my name.

3

1934–1936: Grudziądz
Cavalry Training Centre

In September 1934, I arrived in Grudziądz and reported to the Cavalry Training Centre and to the Officer Cadet School. I was most impressed by the imposing administrative buildings and living quarters. Thirty colleagues who had qualified from Różana arrived at the same time as I, along with some thirty from the three Cadet Corps Schools and another thirty, or so, from the Cavalry Reserve Officer Cadet School [*SPR Kawalerii*]. I will not go into details of quartering, uniform and weapons at this point. All these matters, as well as other logistics, were dealt with by the School's permanent staff comprising a Sergeant Major and a few non-commissioned officers.

The first roll-call was called by the Sergeant Major who reported to Captain Szumski[10] of the 20th Lancers Regiment. The latter then informed us that our year had been named after the Charge of Rokitna. The daring charge of the 2nd Squadron, commanded by Captain Zbigniew Dunin-Wąsowicz[11] went down in the annals of history. In a short speech, he told us what awaited us that year. He introduced the officers: Lieutenant Pawełczak[12] of the 2nd Grochowski Lancers

---

10 Bogumił Szumski (1896–1957) – Cavalry Captain from 1929. In 1932, assigned for service in the Grudziądz Cavalry Officer Cadet Training School. Promoted to the rank of Major in 1936. According to OdB as at 23 March 1939, seconded to the Infantry Training Centre in Rembertów, where he held the position of lecturer. In September 1939, in the rank of Major (service assignment to Reserves Centre of the Suwałki and Podlasie Cavalry Brigade). According to personnel records of the 2nd (Cadre) Armoured Grenadiers Division at 7 December 1943, in the rank of Lt. Colonel as Second-in-Command of the 16th (Cadre) Armoured Brigade. Awarded the Virtuti Militari Order, V Class, the Cross of Independence, Cross of Valour, Gold Cross of Merit and Silver Cross of Merit. Brother of the authoress, Maria Dąbrowska.

11 13 June 1915. From early morning, the II Polish Legions Brigade fought in the area of the village of Rokitna (now in the Ukraine). Captain-of-Horse Zbigniew Dunin-Wąsowicz commanded two squadrons of the Brigade's cavalry. Not waiting for the units which were to reinforce him, he personally headed a charge by the 2nd Squadron. "Taken by surprise by the Charge at Rokitna, the Russians did not manage to hold the Squadron in their first advance positions, then in their second positions until, finally, the charge was broken as a result of heavy losses sustained before the third Russian defence line. The six Lancers remaining from the Squadron turned from these positions into the valley of the Rokitnianka, leaving several dozens of dead and wounded Lancers on the field of battle, among them Captain Wąsowicz." (*Encyklopedia wojskowa [Military Encyclopaedia]*, ed. O. Laskowski, vol. 7, Warsaw 1939, pg. 232).

12 Zygmunt Pawełczak (born 1902) – Cavalry Lieutenant from 1931. In 1932 seconded to the 2nd

Regiment was responsible for the 1st Platoon, Lieutenant Lucjan Pruszyński[13] of the 10th Mounted Rifles Regiment – the 2nd Platoon (mine), and Lieut. Cetnerowski[14] of the 26th Lancers Regiment – the 3rd Platoon. The Sergeant-Major's surname was Wietrzykowski. During a gathering in 2009[15], when someone asked me if I had known Sergeant-Major Wietrzykowski, I was able to tell him all about the Sergeant.

There were two annual intakes in the Officer Cadet Training School – one older and one younger. Relations between them were friendly. Those in my year had come here from all over Poland and we had attended various schools but there were no regional divisions between us, nor better or worse schools.

Standard dormitories contained six beds. I was assigned to a small dormitory which I shared with two colleagues during the two years of my stay in the Officer Cadet Training School: with Zbyszek Zieliński[16] from Warsaw, who had completed schooling at one of the three Cadet Corps Schools in Poland, and with Józio Rymel[17] from Grudziądz, who had joined us from the Cavalry Reserve

Lancers Regiment. In 1938, promoted to the rank of Captain. According to OdB as at 23 March 1939 service assignment to the 2nd Lancers Regiment. According to personnel data on 2 December 1942, held the rank of Captain as Commander of the 2nd Squadron of the Motorised Rifles Battalion (one of the rifle battalions of the 1st Armoured Brigade before its re-organisation, formed on the order of the Supreme Commander dated 26 February 1942 from the Reconnaissance Unit of the 10th Armoured Cavalry Brigade and part of the Corps' Heavy Machine Gun Battalion). "This battalion, assigned to the 10th Armoured Cavalry Brigade was soon renamed the 10th Dragoon Battalion; it was divided into squadrons in such a way that it stopped being classed as infantry." (*Piechota 1939–1945* [Infantry 1939-1945] 1972, file 9/10, pg. 102); "[...] The 2nd Training Company consisted of five or six high school classes and around eight secondary school classes, a total of about 300 pupils. Captain Zygmunt Pawełczak was appointed its commander; he was a pre-war instructor in the Grudziądz Cavalry Officer Cadet Training Centre and later – in Scotland – an officer of the 10th Dragoon Regiment of the 1st Armoured Division" (Z.S. Siemaszko, *I co dalej? [And what next?]* (1945-1948), London–Warsaw 2016, pg. 51).

13   Lucjan Władysław Pruszyński (1904–1970) – Cavalry 2nd Lieutenant from 1931. In 1932 assigned to the 10th Cavalry Rifles Regiment. In 1938, promoted to Captain in the Cavalry Officers' Corps. According to OdB on 23 marca 1939, Mobilisation Officer in the Reconnaissance Unit of the 10th Cavalry Brigade. Awarded the Cross of Valour four times, the Silver Cross of Merit with Swords, the Monte Cassino Cross, the Gold Medal of the National Treasury of the Republic of Poland, as well as other Polish, English and French awards. After the war, Deputy-Chairman of the Committee of the National Treasury of the Republic of Poland for the State of Michigan. Distinguished Polish activist in the United States. Died in Detroit and was buried there in Mount Olivet Cemetery.

14   Julian Cetnerowski (1903–1940) – Cavalry Lieutenant from 1932. In 1932, assigned to the 26th Lancers Regiment. In September 1939, Commander of the 2nd Squadron, the 26th Lancers Regiment. Wounded at Hussaków on 30 September 1939. Imprisoned by the Soviets in Starobielsk. Murdered in Kharkov.

15   Since 1989, the Council of the Foundation for the Preservation of the Traditions of Polish Cavalry has been organising reunions of cavalrymen of the II Republic of Poland and these take place in Grudziądz.

16   Zbigniew Henryk Zieliński (1913–1940) – graduated from the Officer Cadet Training School in Grudziądz in the rank of 2nd Lieutenant in 1936. According to OdB on 23 March 1939, Platoon Commander in the 1st Light Cavalry Regiment with the rank of Lieutenant.

17   Józef Stanisław Rymel (born 1914) – graduated from the Officer Cadet Training School in Grudziądz

Officer Cadet School. We came from different parts of Poland and from three different schools, yet, during the two years we spent together, we never had any arguments. In fact, as émigrés, Józio Rymel and I were on friendly terms until his departure from London.

No matter which schools we attended before arriving in Grudziądz, we carried out the same exercises and were treated equally. If it turned out that there were differences in our training to-date (for instance, Józio in horse-riding), they were quickly evened out and disappeared. Any rivalry had a strictly positive nature. We were young and tried to carry out all the exercises to the best of our ability – if nothing else then to get better marks.

The day started with reveille at 6 o'clock, and we marched out to the stables and groomed the horses. In the winter, instead of marching we would usually run to warm ourselves, singing a song about "Heartless Kasia who chased her cattle out at dawn". Grooming the horses was a complicated task and we had much to learn. The grooming tasks over, we would return to the barracks where we had breakfast and then went to our morning classes. These classes were aimed at widening the scope of the knowledge we had acquired earlier. For me and my colleagues from the Cadet Corps Schools, horse-riding and vaulting were a novelty. Vaulting is a form of riding while performing various acrobatics on a horse, cantering around the instructor. During our first riding lessons, we rode without spurs. It was only when the instructor decided that we had a good understanding of the horse and that the horse understood us and reacted to our heel and thigh signals, and when he was confident we would not hurt the horse, that we were given permission to wear spurs. This was a promotion of sorts.

Breakfasts and suppers were served in our own dining rooms, whilst dinners were eaten in the mess together with our older colleagues. It was a tradition that we all stood to greet the school head boy, chosen from the older year, and only sat down when he sat. And the same with eating. Smoking was allowed once he had lit up or given us his permission to do so.

The Royal Court

As the week's working days were full of classes and Saturdays or Sundays occasionally entailed guard duty or some other duties, it is hardly surprising that, when a free Saturday came round, we would look for somewhere to go and enjoy ourselves. Grudziądz had plenty to offer us. There was a variety of entertainment

with the rank of 2nd Lieutenant in 1936. According to OdB on 23 March 1939, Platoon Commander in the 20th Lancers Regiment with the rank of Lieutenant.

available, such as theatres, cinemas, coffee houses and dance halls. The most popular of these was the Royal Court. This was an elegant venue with a very specific atmosphere. It was not possible not to enjoy oneself!

Naturally, the biggest attraction of the Royal Court was the presence of Grudziądz's young ladies. Charming young women would go there in order to meet young, elegant Officer Cadets. After some time, we got together with a group of such young ladies and would meet with them on Saturdays on an informal basis, without having to make prior arrangements. There were other groups, too, which would meet just the one evening, make friends and have a good time together. There were no lasting relationships, nor romances. There may have been a few tears towards the end of the academic year but there were no broken hearts. I can honestly say that, throughout my two-years in Grudziądz, there were no major misunderstandings or scandals.

'Dyatka', our Guardian-Gran'pa

A tradition which probably dated to the very beginnings of the School was the choice of Guardian-Gran'pa [Polish: *Dziadek* but here pronounced with a soft second 'd' as in Russian – *Dyatka*]. Poles seem to favour foreign influences. A first-year officer cadet would choose a 'Guardian' from the ranks of the older officer cadets who was known as *Dyatka*, [English: Gran'pa]. On arrival in Grudziądz, even those who had never heard of this tradition, soon learned of it.

Both school years were quartered in the same building and so we would frequently visit each other. Common interests led to more frequent encounters and thus stronger friendships were forged. The younger officer cadet could thus judge when the situation was ripe enough to allow him to approach an older officer cadet, asking him to be his 'guardian'.

'Sugub'

Sugub was the nickname given to first-year officer cadets. On meeting a younger colleague, a second-year cadet officer might turn to him, saying "Hey, sugub, how are you?" Or, if the younger officer cadet had done something wrong, he might use a harsher tone: "Sugub, don't you know that a sugub should salute an older colleague?" However, if the situation was even more serious, he might address the first-year officer cadet formally by rank: "Officer-Cadet ... ".

A second-year officer cadet could, for example, praise a correct answer or a good deed. The first-year cadet would then reply: "For the greater glory of the Fatherland, Cadet Officer, Sir." A second-year cadet officer could also mete out punishment to a younger colleague, if an answer was incorrect. The lowest degree of punishment was a "squat" (one, two, or more).

Questions varied, one question might be "What is the name of my horse?" Or it could be more frivolous, for instance: "What's the name of my (usually imaginary) fiancée?" As was common in the army, such methods of discipline were intended to keep a soldier on his toes, both mentally and physically, in his everyday behaviour, actions and appearance. More about this later.

Cukanie, or prying, questioning

What is meant by *cukanie*? This is a difficult question because I do not know the origin of the word *cukanie*, nor in which language it had the connotation 'to pry, to question'. In the Grudziądz Cavalry Training Centre, the word was universally used both by the officer cadets and by those in charge, although some of the officer cadets did not approve of the tradition and did not take part. They considered that it was not right to intrude on the private and sometimes intimate matters of the younger officer cadets. Today, we would probably consider it to be an encroachment on "personal rights". Everyone had the right to refrain from this practice. Most of those who did practice it, did so in good part, without giving offence. *Cukanie*, then, was a tradition among the older officer cadets. Personally, I think it was a good one.[18]

Exercises, practicals

Part of our training involved two-week placements and summer manoeuvres in regiments chosen at the beginning of the first year. In my case, this was the 14th Jazłowiecki Lancers Regiment in Lwów.

During the placement period, whether as a corporal or a platoon leader, I took part in normal exercises but socially I was treated as an officer – perhaps not in the first year but in the second, as a warrant officer now, I took my meals in the officers' mess. I had the opportunity to acquaint myself with the officers with whom I was to meet and work in the future. I was acquiring new and practical experiences.

Visits to my home town of Brzeżany at Christmas and Easter were just as exciting, if not more so. It is impossible to define the joy I felt at the prospect of

---

18 The author of the memoirs does not explain how this Lancers' tradition of '*cukanie*', or prying, actually worked. Anyone interested in this tradition and also in the relations between a 'sugub' and a 'Dyatka' may wish to read the blog on: *Wachmistrzowe pogderanki* (http://wachmistrz.blog.onet. pl/2007/04/17/o-ulanskiem-cukaniu/, 16 III 2016) (note, A.Ś.-J.).

relaxing in my home environment – at least for a short while – and seeing the friends, both male and female, with whom I had grown up.

I shall never forget the Easter holidays in 1936. I set off together with Zbyszek Belina-Prażmowski.[19] He was going to Lwów, where his father, Colonel Władysław Belina-Prażmowski, was the Provincial Governor, and I was heading for Brzeżany. As we approached Lwów, Zbyszek suggested that I stop off in Lwów for a day and he would ask his father to take us somewhere for a proverbial 'glass of wine'.

When I arrived the following day at the address I had been given, Zbyszek briefly introduced me to his father. I remember that I was overwhelmed by that meeting – a meeting with history and with a legend. I remember that we went to the Atlas Wine Bar where we chatted while drinking a glass of wine and nibbling almonds. The Colonel knew Brzeżany very well: its inhabitants, the Sieniawski family and the castle. In fact, he knew Brzeżany far better than I, because our history teacher had never taken us to the castle, and our history lessons began with the reign of Poland's first king, Mieszko I, and not with the [Polish] Legions [and the run up to independence]. Even today, I regret that I never learnt the real story of the 'Seven-man patrol'.[20]

Farewell to Grudziądz

The clock moved forward slowly but inexorably and soon it would be time to bid farewell to Grudziądz, the School and my colleagues. Before then, however, we were all faced with a terrible shock when the list of assignments to regiments was announced.

We were faced with a breach of a tradition lasting many years. All our secondments were changed and, instead of assignment to the 14th Jazłowiecki Lancers Regiment, I found myself seconded to the 19th Wołyń Lancers Regiment.

---

19 Zbigniew Władysław Belina-Prażmowski (1914–1937) – graduated from the Grudziądz Cavalry Training School in the rank of 2nd Lieutenant in 1936. He died tragically as a result of a firearms' accident.

20 Władysław Zygmunt Belina-Prażmowski (1888–1938) – from 1909, a member of the Association of Active Combat. As an officer of the Assocation, sent by Commander Józef Piłsudski to France, Belgium and Switzerland where he set up successive units of the Association in Polish communities. "On 2 VIII 1914 sets out on the orders of the Commandant-General, Józef Piłsudski, as leader of a patrol to hinder the Russian mobilization in the Miechów area. After his return on 6 VIII he went out into the field at the head of a cavalry patrol consisting of 6 riflemen, as a reconnaissance unit of the First Cadre Company in its march on Kielce. During the advance, he organised a cavalry platoon which was soon transformed from a platoon into a squadron, then a division and finally, in 1916, into the 1st Lancers Regiment." (*Mała encyklopedia wojskowa [The Small Military Encyclopaedia]*, ed. O. Laskowski, vol. 1, Warsaw 1930, pg. 245).

It is difficult to describe what went on in our minds, in the school ... Everything was in turmoil – preparations for the passing out ceremony, parades etc. I still recall that I was unable to devote any time to my elder brother Kazimierz, who was an officer in the 14th Infantry Regiment and whom I had invited to my promotion ceremony.

All the tasks involved in our departure – visits to stores, return of equipment, arms and so on filled our time to such a degree that we soon forgot about the temporary disappointment caused by changes in assignments. We said our goodbyes to all the staff: the non-commissioned officers, the service staff and the instructors with whom we were on good terms. We bade farewell to our Sergeant Major Wietrzykowski with particular sincerity. He had been helpful to us in all manner of situations. We liked him for his positive and tactful approach to us (I will return to him later).

At the same time, preparations for the passing-out ceremony were in full swing. In line with established tradition, the programme started off with Holy Mass in the Cathedral, attended by school children, colour parties, army units and inhabitants of Grudziądz, culminating in a parade on the Błonie Common. This was followed by a joint dinner with the instructors in our mess.

This emotive day concluded with a grand ball in the Royal Court restaurant. General Wieniawa Długoszowski[21] took part in our revelry and immediately introduced a jovial atmosphere by announcing: "I'll drink informally with you so that I can call each of you by name." The party continued into the early hours.

After all these emotional experiences, we needed a day or two to rest, pack our things and prepare for departure. Equipped with relevant train tickets and orders to report on a specific day and time in a new town and a new regiment, we parted, setting off in different directions, not knowing whether we would ever return to Grudziądz ...

Even the longest vacation must come to an end
Then came the day when I had to take my leave of my father, my brothers and sister, my friends, the Brzeżany Lake, excursions to the country and, in accordance with orders received in Grudziądz, report on a given day to the regiment to which I had been assigned in Ostróg on the River Horyń.

A Lancer was waiting for me at the station in Zdołbunów. He greeted me with a military salute and with a light, sports carriage drawn by two chestnuts

---

21 Bolesław Ignacy Florian Długoszowski-Wieniawa (1881–1942) – Commander of the 2nd Cavalry Division. He was promoted to the rank of Lieutenant General in May 1938.

with glistening black harnesses. The journey to Ostróg did not take long and was brightened by descriptions of various places of interest on the way. The barracks, located on both sides of the main road and constructed in a grey-green brick with red embellishments, made a good impression on me, as did the officers' and non-commissioned officers' buildings (living quarters). I was later to learn that living on a barracks campus without the attractions provided by a town environment meant that we tried to make our stay as pleasant as possible in other ways, by organising picnics and joint excursions. The regiment had a friendly, family atmosphere. The differences between older and younger officers were levelled out. To a great degree this was thanks to the individual commanders of the regiment.

During a short meeting with the Adjutant, I learned that, due to the lack of bachelor's quarters, I was to be billeted privately near the barracks in the home of Mr and Mrs Krupczyński. Mr Krupczyński was an employee of the local prison; he had a wife and daughter.

The following day I reported to the Regimental Commander, Colonel Aleksander Piotraszewski.[22] After a short conversation I was assigned to the 2nd Squadron, commanded by Captain Stanisław Bedryjowski[23], who had originally served in the 2nd Regiment of the Polish Legions, although he had not taken part in the charge at Rokitna. However, we struck up a warm relationship which was to last into our time in exile. My second-in-command was Platoon Leader Tomasik. He selected a duty horse for me – a good-tempered dark bay called Bojka. Later I was given an equestrian chestnut mare called Diana, which I trained with a great deal of help from an older colleague, Wojtek Gumiński[24] (killed in action in the September 1939 Campaign).

Tomasik chose Eugeniusz Wensak to be my groom and he looked after my

---

22   Aleksander Piotraszewski (1890–1980) – Cavalry Lieutenant Colonel from 1928. In 1932 Commander of the 19th Wołyń Lancers Regiment, named after Gen. Edmund Różycki. Awarded the Order of Virtuti Militari V Class, the Independence Cross, the Cross of Valour and the Gold Cross of Merit. Held the rank of Colonel from 1933. According to OdB on 23 March 1939, held the rank of Colonel and Chairman of Rebuilding Committee No. 2 Poznań. Buried in the Morąg Cemetery.

23   Stanisław Florian Bedryjowski (1897–1973) – regular service Captain in the Cavalry as of 1930. According to OdB on 23 March 1939, rank of Cavalry Captain in the Corps Sector No. 1 – Warsaw Staff Command. Seconded to 2nd Rokitniański Light Cavalry Regiment and 19th Lancers Regiment. According to Death Notices, Colonel, or Lieutenant Colonel of Cavalry. Awarded the Cross of Independence, Cross of Valour (4 times) and other Polish and foreign decorations. Died in London and buried in Putney Vale Cemetery.

24   Wojciech Gumiński (1912–1939) – 2nd Lieutenant of Cavalry from 1935; subsequently promoted to the rank of Lieutenant in the Cavalry in 1939. According to OdB on 23 March 1939, Platoon Commander in the 4th Squadron of the 19th Lancers Regiment. In September 1939, Commander of the 4th Squadron of the 19th Wołyń Lancers Regiment, named after Gen. Edmund Różycki. Killed in action on 13 September at Battle of Dębe Wielkie.

horse – groomed, fed and saddled it, held it whilst I was dismounting. Wensak was conscripted into the Regiment in 1936. In 1937, he attended Non-Comissioned Officer Training and a year later returned to the Platoon. We escaped together when the Germans surprised us on the border and we parted company at the Hungarian border guard post. Following a successful escape from the internment camp for rank and file troops, he joined me at the beginning of 1940 – in April or May – in France, in the Reconnaissance Unit of the 3rd Infantry Division. Wensak was evacuated to Great Britain with me and later we were both in the Polish Resettlement Corps [PKPR].[25] On demobilisation in 1947, he ran a horticultural farm in Esher, where he lived. He used to visit me in East Molesey, and I would visit him during the strawberry season. He had a wife and three children. We were all good friends.

I will not go into details of my work in the Regiment because that can be found in the regulations which have been preserved. During my first visit to the stables, I met the four-legged veteran, Medzio. Medzio was Major Feliks Jaworski's combat mount and had accompanied him in all the battles and skirmishes in Wołyń and – like his master – Medzio, too, had been wounded several times. As I have mentioned previously, Medzio was a grace and favour guest of the Regiment until September 1939.

---

25 For Polish Resettlement Corps (PKPR) see: pg. 92.

4

1938: Changes

Over a period of three years, changes took place in the Regiment's command. In 1937, Colonel Piotraszewski left and in 1938 the Regiment was put under the temporary command of Colonel Dezyderiusz Zawistowski[26] for a year. When the latter retired before September, the Regiment came under the command of Colonel Pętkowski[27] – a member of the post-Piłsudski's Legion generation.

In London in 1941, before my departure for West Africa, I briefly met the previous commander, Colonel Lewiński.[28] To a great extent, it is to these commanders that we owed the family atmosphere and friendly relationships in the Regiment. And so, while I did not lose my affection for Lwów itself, I had no reason to yearn for the 14th Jazłowiecki Lancers Regiment.[29]

In 1938, on the strength of Ministry of Defence recommendations, a decisive change took place in my cavalry platoon: it was transformed into a cycle platoon in the summer, and a skiing platoon in the winter.

---

26 Dezyderiusz Jan Jerzy Zawistowski (1891–1939) – with the regular cavalry officer rank of Major (Engineer) in 1928. In 1932, seconded to the 19th Wołyń Lancers Regiment, named after Gen. Edmund Różycki. Holder of the Virtuti Militari Order V Class, Cross of Independence, Cross of Valour (twice) and Gold Cross of Merit. On 31 March 1939, retired from active duty with the rank of Lieutenant Colonel. Killed in action on 20 September at Kamionka Strumiłowa and buried there.

27 Józef Zygmunt Pętkowski (1894–1940) – regular Cavalry Major from 1928. In 1932 seconded to the 7th Horse Rifles Regiment. Next, in the Armed Forces' General Inspectorate. Awarded the Cross of Independence, the Cross of Valour (twice) and the Silver Cross of Merit. In 1933, promoted to the rank of Lieutenant Colonel. Acording to OdB on 23 March 1939, seconded to the 19th Lancers Regiment where he served as Regimental Commander. In September 1939, he commanded the 19th Wołyń Lancers Regiment. Imprisoned by the Russians in Starobielsk. Murdered in Kharkov.

28 Zbigniew Wincenty Brochwicz-Lewiński (1877–1951) – regular service Colonel in the Cavalry Oficers' Corps from 1927. Awarded the Order of Virtuti Militari V Class, the Cross of Independence, the Polonia Restituta Order IV Class, Cross of Valour (four times) and the Gold Cross of Merit. According to OdB on 23 March 1939, seconded to the General Inspectorate of the Armed Forces where he held the position of officer responsible for Military Horse Training. He died as a result of a tragic accident in Glasgow and was buried in Dalbeth Cemtery in Glasgow.

29 "As we envisaged, the day was sunny and hot. We lay on the grassy verge of the river, lazily watching the River Wilia which was teeming with people and kayaks. Attractive young female students from Lwów and from Warsaw sauntered along the riverside in their tight-fitting swimming costumes, accompanied by local girls – that year's contingent of school-leavers. Bolek Szukiewicz and Tadzio Bączkowski cantered across the meadow on their splendid cavalry mounts, looking out for young ladies with whom to spend the evening." (M. Święcicki, *Pasażer na gapę. Opowiadania [Free Rider. Tales]*, London 1983, pg. 65).

The concept of motorisation of the Polish Army had been considered by staff commands for many years. Its development was limited by Poland's economic situation. In 1938, two regiments were motorised – the 24th Lancers Regiment and the 10th Mounted Rifles Regiment.[30] Cycle squadrons were introduced into brigades and cycle platoons into regiments. As I had undergone a skiing course after leaving Grudziądz, I was appointed commander of a cycle platoon (in the summer) and a ski platoon (in the winter).[31]

Basically, nothing much changed. We continued to carry out field exercises, the only difference being that now, instead of horses, we rode cycles. Cycling did not present a problem as most Lancers remembered this skill from childhood. The uniform terrain surrounding the barracks facilitated cycle training in the summer and skiing training in the winter. Thankfully, everything ran smoothly and there were no serious accidents.

---

30 These regiments were motorised in May 1937.
31 More about the development, changes in organisation and nature of Cavalry training before the outbreak of WW2, see: E. Kozłowski, *Wojsko Polskie 1936–1939. Próby modernizacji i rozbudowy [The Polish Army 1936-1939. Attempts at Modernisation and Expansion]*, Warsaw 1974, pg. 144–162.

5

1939

The political situation continued to worsen and when Russian talks with the West broke down and Russia signed a Pact with Hitler, it became obvious that war was imminent. The West stopped us from announcing a general mobilisation claiming that Hitler would see this as a declaration of war on the part of Poland, and then the West would not be obliged to come to our aid.[32]

When mobilisation was announced, I happened to be in the company of the White Russian Association. I made for the barracks at a run. Mobilisation was carried out efficiently and according to plan and the Regiment was transported by rail to the region where Army 'Łódź' was concentrated and we took up positions in the Mokra-Miedźno area. The task facing the entire Polish front was to halt and delay German troops which had been moving eastwards for two weeks. During this period, the Allies were to mount their attack and hamper the German onslaught on the Polish front. No assault came from the West. Poland blocked the German onslaught for much longer than two weeks. Moving from one position of resistance to another, we generally travelled on foot, cross-country. The roads teemed with civilian refugees and army units (mostly artillery). During a march from one position to another, a Head Forester from Poznań, Dr Leon

---

32 Plans for the development of the Army envisaged that Poland would field 30 infantry divisions, 9 infantry reserve divisions, 2 highland brigades, 11 cavalry brigades and 2 motorised brigades (including 1 in the process of organisation). On 1 September 1939, 14 infantry divisions were in place, as well as 2 infantry reserve divisions, 2 highland brigades, 6 cavalry brigades and 1 motorised brigade. During transportation to assigned positions, there were 5 infantry divisions and 3 cavalry brigades, and as reserves for the Supreme Commander there were 7 infantry divisions, 2 infantry reserve divisions and 1 cavalry brigade. During mobilisation there were 2 infantry divisions, 2 infantry reserve divisions and 1 infantry brigade, and as reserves for the Supreme Commander there were initially 2 infantry divisions and later 3 infantry reserve divisions and 1 motorised brigade – of these, 2 reserve infantry divisions could not be mobilised and only a few battalions were active. When compared to the situation in France in 1940, where the process of mobilisation and concentration was fully completed under excellent conditions, in Poland only 75 percent of the planned mobilisation was completed: "under Allied diplomatic pressure, mobilisation was postponed twice", (PISM, A.XII.62/45, *Wojskowe Biuro Propagandy i Oświaty. Kampania wojenna we wrześniu i październiku 1939 r. w Polsce [Army Propaganda and Education Office. The military campaign in September and October 1939 in Poland]*); compare: *Polskie Siły Zbrojne w II wojnie światowej [Polish Armed Forces in WW2]*, vol. 1: *Kampania wrześniowa 1939 [The September Campaign 1939]*, part. 1: *Polityczne i wojskowe położenie Polski przed wojną [Poland's political and military situation before the war]*, London 1951, pg. 289–477).

Ossowski[33] joined my platoon. As the President's Head Gamekeeper, he used to organise hunts for VIPs visiting Poland. He had many an interesting tale about these hunting parties. The friendship we struck up during that march lasted until his death, many years later in London.

During one of our successive changes of position a man came up to me and recounted the dream he had had the previous night. In his dream, he saw a large, beautiful red rose. Suddenly, the petals began to fall away from the rose. Only the middle was left, and new petals began to grow from it. They, too, were red. Soon there was a whole rose but now it was smaller. His interpretation of the dream was that we would lose this war but Poland would re-emerge, albeit smaller. And, indeed, that is what happened – Poland lost Lwów, Wilno and also the "Charm of Polesie".[34]

During the next change of positions, I met an elderly man who had studied in Berlin and Vienna during the 1930s and, along with others, had listened to Hitler's speeches. Opinions as to Hitler were varied. The older generation considered him a madman, while the younger people believed that he would save and rebuild Germany. Young people were very pro-Hitler.

---

33 Leon Ossowski (1905–1960) – until 1939, Head Forester of the State Forests, Pomorze Province Gamekeeper. He lectured on the conservation of forests and hunting; editor-in-chief of the monthly *Myśliwy* [Hunter]. Co-organiser of the Polish Pavilion in the International Hunting Exhibition in Berlin in 1937. Before the outbreak of the Second World War, he published a book entitled *Choroby zwierzyny łownej [Diseases of Game Species],* and also published over fifty works on the subject of forestry, biology and hunting in Polish, German and French journals. Several times Chairman and Fellow of the *Baltia* Alumni Corporation of the University of Poznań. During the war, he served in Poland, France and Great Britain (18th Pomorski Lancers Regiment). In June 1940, he arrived in Scotland from France. On demobilisation from the army, he was appointed Head of the Forestry Commission in the Ministry of Reconstruction of Public Administration and subsequently Head of the Forestry Commission in the Department of Industry and Trade in London. A Government Delegate to the FAO (Food and Agriculture Organisation of the United Nations) in Washington. After the war, Ossowski was technical advisor to the Scottish Landowners Co-operative Forestry Society in Edinburgh and a Research Specialist in the Union Department of Forestry in South Africa. In 1960, he was appointed Chief Entomologist and Head of the Department of Entomology in the Wattle Research Institute, University of Natal in South Africa. That same year he chaired the Virus Research Section and was responsible for the organisation of a symposium on the subject of viruses at the XI International Entomology Congress in Vienna. From the outbreak of the Second World War to 1960, Ossowski published some forty works on the subject of forest conservation, entomology, biology and forestry in English, American, German and Czech journals. During the period 1942 and 1943, he won competitions held by the Royal Scottish Forestry Society for papers on the subject of forestry and forest conservation. He died in London. In accordance with the wishes of the deceased, his funeral took place in Aberdeen, his wife's family home.

34 The tango *Polesia czar* [The *Charm of Polesie – Polesie being a province in the eastern borderlands – translator's note*], first appeared in 1936 (some sources give the date as 1939). It was one of the biggest hits of the late 1930s. The author and composer, Jerzy Artur Kostecki, had spent a holiday there in a country estate in the 1920s. In contemporary times this Tango was popularised by Krzysztof Klenczon (note: A.Ś.-J.).

As we approached Warsaw, Colonel Pętkowski summoned me and said: "I am informed that all the bridges on the River Vistula have been destroyed or damaged. The Regiment will have to swim across the river, you and your cyclists won't be able to do that. You'll have to find your own means of crossing." Unfortunately, he did not tell me where the Regiment intended to cross, or where to look for it. The following day, after completing preparations, I headed away from the Regiment and, despite later attempts, I never managed to regain contact with it.

I reached Warsaw without any incidents and crossed the River Vistula over the Poniatowski Bridge. In the Saska Kępa district, I met Major Sienkiewicz[35] of the 2nd Grochowski Lancers Regiment who told me that he had been ordered to collect together all the small, lost units and individual soldiers, and that he would try to find out where my Regiment was headed. In the meantime, he ordered me and my platoon to Mińsk Mazowiecki.

In the barracks of the 7th Lancers Regiment in Mińsk Mazowiecki, we found sufficient horses and harnesses so that my platoon, which by now had increased to the size of a squadron, abandoned its cycles for horses and was transformed into a cavalry squadron.[36] Here I met a reserve officer, Second Lieutenant Zygmunt Godyń[37] who, like Leon Ossowski, joined my platoon (after the war in our émigré

---

35 Józef Sienkiewicz (1898–1985) – born in the Ukraine. In November 1917, he presented himself in Antoniny in the Wołyń Province where the 2nd Lancers Regiment was being formed as part of the I Polish Corps, commanded by General Józef Dowbor-Muśnicki. With this regiment, he took part in the 1918-1920 war. Promoted to the rank of Captain in 1924. Awarded the Cross of Valour (4 times), and the Silver Cross of Merit. In 1932, seconded to the 2nd Lancers Regiment. Student of the Military Academy. On graduation, Chief-of-Staff of General Ludwik Kmicic-Skrzyński's Cavalry Brigade with the rank of Major. Prior to September 1939, Second-in-Command of the 2nd Lancers Regiment. From 15 September, he commanded the 41st Infantry Division's divisional cavalry which had been formed that day. According to his membership record in the Secretarial Office of Unit Associations (2nd Grochowski Lancers Regiment): "After the September Campaign, I was taken prisoner by the Germans on 8 X 1939 – wounded on the Hungarian border. I was held in Oflag VII A Murnau POW camp." When the war was over, he devoted himself to cultural and historic activities. Worked as a volunteer in the Polish Institute and Gen. Sikorski Museum in London. He provided both financial and moral support to the Colours' Foundation. Created a room in the Museum dedicated to the preservation of mementoes of the 2nd Lancers Regiment. Died in London. The ashes of the late Józef Sienkiewicz and his wife (a soldier of the AK Underground Resistance Army) were laid to rest in a cemetery in Suwałki, at the foot of a monument dedicated to the 2nd Grochowski Lancers Regiment.
36 When comparing his memoirs of his military service with archival material (here and further on) we find many discrepancies and mistakes made by the author. However, bearing in mind his age when he set down his recollections, this is not surprising.
37 Zygmunt Paweł Godyń (1910–1979) – Lwów Technical University, graduate in forestry. Member of the Cavalry Officer Reserve Corps with the rank of 2nd Lieutenant from 1934 (assigned to service with the 6th Kaniowski Lancers Regiment in Stanisławów). Completed a squadron commanders' course for reserve officers. In September 1939, Platoon Commander in the 22nd Podkarpacki Lancers Regiment, reached France via Hungary. He was seconded to the 4th Infantry Division which was being formed at the time. According to personnel records of the 7th Cadre Rifles Brigade dated 21 November 1940,

community our acquaintanceship turned into a permanent friendship which lasted until his death). After two or three days, we left Mińsk Mazowiecki and set off in an easterly direction. We were joined by a squadron of the 22nd Lancers Regiment (I do not remember the name of its commander). On 12 September 1939, we reached the environs of Zamość.

March towards the Hungarian border

On 17 September, despite lack of communication, we found out that the Bolsheviks had crossed our borders. We also received news of an order given by the Supreme Commander, Marshal Rydz-Śmigły, which I quote *verbatim*: "I order that all troops make a break-through in small units or individually to Romania or Hungary, and from there to France where the Polish Army will be re-formed; if anyone does not want to go into exile but prefers to return and take care of his family, he can be discharged."[38] From my platoon, only my second-in-command, Sergeant Major Jan Dłużyński requested that he be discharged. He said that he wished to return to his family and Major Sienkiewicz let him go. It was not until many, many years later that I learnt that Dłużyński had managed to reach his family safely.

The Squadron Commander – a Captain-of-Horse who had joined us – now

Second-in-Command of the 2nd Platoon of the 7th Anti-tank Company with the rank of Cavalry Reserve 2nd Lieutenant. According to his membership record in the Secretarial Office of Unit Associations dated 1 March 1941, promoted to the rank of Lieutenant of Cavalry. Until 1945, seconded to Bureau II of Polish Army General Staff. In 1945, seconded to the 9th Małopolski Lancers Regiment as Adjutant. Founder and, for many years, editor of *Przegląd Kawalerii i Broni Pancernej* [Cavalry and Armoured Services Review]. Knight of the Polonia Restituta Order. Also awarded the Gold Cross of Merit and other honours. Died in St. Helier Hospital in Carshalton, Surrey; buried in London's Gunnersbury Cemetery. (For more information, see: G. Łukomski, *Ułan i strażnik kawaleryjskiej pamięci. Rotmistrz Zygmunt Godyń 1910–1979 [Lancer and Guardian of Cavalry Traditions. Captain-of-Horse Zygmunt Godyń 1910-1979]*, Poznań – Warsaw – London 2015).

38 "Soldiers! The Bolshevik invasion of Poland took place while our armies were carrying out a manoeuvre aimed at concentrating our forces in the south-eastern part of Poland to enable provision of supplies and military equipment, and to open up communication and liaison via Romania with France and England, to enable us to carry on fighting. The Soviet invasion prevented us from carrying out this plan. All our forces capable of continuing the fight were involved in action against the Germans. Under the circumstances, I felt that it was my duty to avoid unnecessary bloodshed in combatting the Soviets and to save what can still be saved. The shots fired by the Border Defence Corps at the Bolsheviks as they crossed the border were proof of the fact that we were not giving up our territories willfully. And since the Soviets did not fire on our units on the first day, nor did they disarm them, I judged that it would be possible to carry out a gradual withdrawal of a substantial part of our forces across the border to Romanian and Hungarian territories. I wanted to do this so that you could then be transported to France where the Polish Army could be regrouped. I was anxious that the Polish Soldier be able to continue to take part in the war and that, having achieved a victorious conclusion, the Polish Army would continue to exist and to represent Poland and Poland's interests. You must bear in mind this most important aim" (PISM, A.II.25/2, document 1, Order of the Supreme Commander, E. Rydz-Śmigły dated 17 September 1939).

declared that he intended to take his squadron and go to the aid of embattled Warsaw; he left us and rode off towards our capital city. The following day mounted and fully armed, our squadron began its march southwards, towards the Hungarian border. We did not have any maps. Having a general grasp of geography, we knew that if we went southwards in a straight line from Zamość, we would reach the point where – prior to September – three borders converged: those of Slovakia, Hungary and Poland.

When the German and Russian units met, both sides retreated a few kilometres – the Germans westwards and the Russians eastwards – thus forming a theoretical no-man's land which was, of course, controlled by both sides.

We decided to carry out our entire march to the south by night from one area of forest to the next. During the march, we used guides: sometimes a forest keeper, sometimes a woman or a young lad who knew the area. This helped us to avoid obstacles. We never entered any village. Taking advantage of the help of local Poles, we crossed the flat terrain almost entirely on foot and had to lead the horses. In this way, we reached the mountain ridge where, according to our calculations, we would find the meeting point of the three borders. To ensure that we would not cross the Slovak border by mistake, we decided to veer a few kilometres to the east and, after crossing the ridge, find ourselves in Hungary.

We now had to pick our way carefully as the horses slid and stumbled on the uneven mountainous terrain. [...] On 10 October, we reached a tiny hamlet of 8-10 cottages. After a full day's march, we decided to stop off to water the horses, loosen their harnesses and take a short rest. We were assured by the inhabitants who, as we later found out, were not Polish, that there were no German or Russian units in the area. We certainly did not expect there to be any active units in an area so remote from the front.

Hardly had we managed to make ourselves comfortable in the few local cottages to dry our clothes and take a rest when a sudden machine gun burst caused us to spring to our feet. I leapt through the door and took in the situation within seconds. I shouted to my colleagues: "Take the back door and head straight for the forest! Wait for me there!" and then joined them myself. The first salvo had missed us because we were all lying down but it had brought us to our feet immediately. The second posed a danger to all those who, like me, had appeared in the doorway, or were still getting dressed.

I immediately realised that the ill-disposed inhabitants of these regions were *Boykos*[39] and that they had summoned a German unit. The Germans had positioned themselves on the road alongside the cottages, lit up the fronts of the cottages with a small floodlight and had opened fired on us.

As soon as I had joined my companions, we began to scramble upwards as fast as we could towards the border. I had no idea why all the others from the rest of the cottages were not doing the same. Those who managed to escape with me were: Leon Ossowski, Second Lieutenant Godyń, Captain Kudelski[40], artillery Captain F. Reiss, a Summary Court Officer (I do not recall his name), Genio Wensak and Platoon Leader Bamburski – there were eight of us in total.

Successive machine gun salvoes raked across the cottages and several Lancers, including Major Sienkiewicz, were wounded. Like all the rest, Major Sienkiewicz spent five years as a prisoner-of-war. It was not until he was freed that I met him in the émigré community. I never did learn whether he had heard my command and, if so, why he had not responded to it. Why had no-one from any of the other cottages joined me – except Bamburski?

We climbed quickly up to the ridge. The barking of dogs – whether local or German, I had no idea – gave us added strength. On the way, we encountered a Hungarian guard who led us to the guard post.

We crossed the border on the night of 10 to 11 October[41] after a march lasting almost an entire month. If I remember correctly, the guard post was called Rusk. The Hungarians welcomed us in a friendly manner. They provided a change of

---

39 *Boykos* – highlanders of Ruthenian and Wallachian [Vlach] origin inhabiting the Eastern Carpathians. After the Second World War, only a small part of the territories where they lived remained within the Polish borders. Most *Boykos* were deported from the Polish People's Republic and re-settled in the Ukrainian Soviet Socialist Republic, or – in accordance with the *Wisła Operation* – were dispersed throughout Poland. (Note: A.Ś.-J.)

40 Bolesław Kudelski (born 1901) – rank of Lieutenant of Infantry from 1923. In 1932, seconded to service in the Border Defence Corps, in the rank of Lieutenant. Next, with rank of Captain from 1936. According to OdB on 23 March 1939, Adjutant to the Commander of the III Battalion, 86th Infantry Regiment. In September 1939, Information Officer in Staff of the 29th Infantry Division. In 1940 in France, Commander of the 2nd Company, IV Battalion of the 2nd Demi-brigade of the Independent Highland Rifles Brigade (according to personnel records of the Independent Highland Rifles Brigade at moment of embarkation). Next, Second-in-Command of 2nd Company, 1st Battalion Highland Rifles (according to personnel records dated 1 November 1940. After 1 June 1945, with the rank of Major seconded to service in the 5th Małopolski Infantry Rifles Battalion, which formed part of the 4th Infantry Division. "This newest and largest Division in the Polish Armed Forces in the West, whose OdB exceeded 21,000 officers and troops, only began to form on 15 February 1945 in Scotland, and was based on the remaining part of the cadre of the Armoured Grenadiers Division, once the 16th Armoured Brigade had been withdrawn and made independent." ("Piechota 1939–1945" [Infantry 1939-1945], 1973, file. 12, pg. 34).

41 Compare with footnote no. 35. Józef Sienkiewicz gives the date as 8 October ("I was taken prisoner by the Germans on 8 X 1939 – wounded on the Hungarian border"). Also, in one of the service files relating to Tadeusz Bączkowski, the date of crossing the Hungarian border is given as 9th October.

clothes, as ours were soaked through, gave us some hot food and we could then rest.

The following day started with formalities: listing names and ranks. The Hungarians gave us the soldier's pay to which we were entitled. I remember that with my entire pay I was able to buy a bar of chocolate. What we had missed the most throughout our entire march was sugar and salt. On the second or third day, the Hungarians segregated us. They sent my Lancers, Wensak and Platoon Leader Bamburski, to a camp for rank and file soldiers, and the rest of us to a camp for officers. That was my second parting with Wensak. I reminded him of the Supreme Commander's order that "our aim is France."[42]

Our group of officers was sent to a place called Dömös, where there was already a considerable group of earlier arrivals. The camp commanders were a retired Hungarian Colonel and a Polish Colonel – I do not remember their names. We were quartered in boarding houses with full board but were greatly disappointed on that first day. We had been told we would be having goulash for supper. In my mind's eye, I had a picture of a Polish goulash – beef in a thick brown sauce. Imagine our disappointment when a pot of steaming broth with bits of meat floating in it was placed on the table. We ate it anyway ...

The main subject of conversation in the camp was escape to France. The first problem was how to get to Budapest and the Consulate, where Colonel Bogoria-Zakrzewski[43] operated under the guise of Consul.

There was no railway station in Dömös itself, the nearest was on the other side of the Danube. There was a Polish camp there, too, and in it was my Platoon Commander from Różana on the Narew, Captain Rozborski. In order to assess the possibility of escape, I decided to get myself transferred there. The guard guided me across the bridge. The Hungarian Commander asked me why I wanted to be transferred, was I being badly treated? I replied that no, I was quite happy

---

42 See also Order issued by Marshal Edward Rydz-Śmigły to the Polish Armed Forces on 20 September 1939, in: *Rumuński azyl. Losy Polaków 1939–1945 [Romanian Asylum. The Fate of Poles 1939-1945]*, research/ed. A. Wancerz-Gluza, Warsaw 2009, pg. 37.

43 Adam Bogoria-Zakrzewski (1892–1958) – from July 1914 to December 1917 in the Russian Army. In 1915, promoted to Second Lieutenant and to Lieutenant a year later. From 23 December 1917 in Gen. Józef Dowbor-Muśnicki's I Corps. In the Polish Army from 1 November 1918. Rank of Major from 1918, Lieutenant Colonel from 1927, Colonel from 1931. In September 1939, commanded the Pomorska Cavalry Brigade in the 'Czersk' Operational Group, part of the 'Pomorze' Army. In October 1939, he broke through to Hungary and in December that same year, arrived in France. Next, now in Great Britain, he commanded the Reserves Training Centre in Crawford and the Broughton [officers'] Camp, reorganised into the 7th Cadre Rifles Brigade, and subsequently assigned to the command of the military staging camp [in Auchtertool]. In March 1946, he returned to Poland. Died in Sopot and buried there.

but that a friend of mine was here and I would like to be with him. I told him who this was. The Camp Commander shook his finger at me and said: "Oh, no ... we don't need any more Rozborskis here – you'll have to go back."

It turned out that Captain Rozborski had escaped from the camp the previous day. So, my escape attempt was unsuccessful. Just as well.

Life in the camp followed a rather humdrum routine. There was no point in making a drama of the tragedy which had befallen us. We spent the evenings in a friendly bar, discussing and drinking wine. I remember one occasion when we reminisced about cavalry traditions. The discussion centred on the 8th Lancers Regiment named after Prince Józef Poniatowski and the 1st Lancers Regiment (*Galizisches Ulanen-Regiment "Ritter von Brudermann" Nr. 1*)[44], in which many Polish officers had served (they were later to be soldiers of the Polish Army). My friend, Leon Ossowski, quoted a well-known song about the 1st Lancers Regiment in German and this caused a great uproar. We were all ordered to report to the Polish Camp Commander.

The matter dragged on and in December we organised an escape to the Consulate in Budapest. There, we were given civilian clothes, money for the journey and a guide who would take us to the Yugoslavian border. The guide led us by a route which enabled us to cross the border at a point in no man's land, near a station where we brought a ticket to Zagreb. In Zagreb, we were met by a contact who drove us to Split. We then had to wait some time for a ship to Marseilles.

The weather in Split was warm and sunny. The sun shone brightly, and the emerald coloured Adriatic sparkled. We were able to move freely around the town but avoided making ourselves conspicuous in large groups. The Yugoslavs were well disposed towards us but there were plenty of German spies on the lookout for "Sikorski's tourists"[45], as we were called. I have pleasant memories of that short stay in Split. On 29 December, we finally reached Marseilles and spent a few days in the *Camp de Carpiagne* camp[46].

---

44 The 8th Prince Józef Poniatowski Lancers Regiment was formed in 1918 after 'complete transfer' of the 1st Austrian Lancers Regiment to service in a newly independent Poland. The first squadron of this regiment had been established 134 years earlier by Prince Poniatowski, at that time an Austrian Major (for more information, see: K. Krzeczunowicz, *Ułani Księcia Józefa. Historia 8 Pułku Ułanów Ks. Józefa Poniatowskiego 1784–1945 [Prince Józef's Lancers. History of the 8th Prince Józef Poniatowski Lancers Regiment 1784-1945]*, London 1960).
45 This was the name given by German propaganda to Polish soldiers making their way to France.
46 Compare page 21 (BACK IN TIME WITH 'ROTMISTRZ' BĄCZKOWSKI).

6

1940: Paris – the barracks in Bessières – verification and assignment

At the beginning of January 1940, I was sent to Paris, to the barracks in Bessières, where verification took place. After the verification procedure, I was sent to a place called Sables d'Or on the English Channel, where the Reserve Centres for the Podolski Brigade and the 9th Lancers Regiment (a group of officers) were stationed.[47]

We were quartered in local boarding houses, with full board. It was here that I came to know the various little sea creatures which were cooked by the staff. For several months, we underwent a period of organisation and re-organisation; we familiarised ourselves with the arms and equipment supplied by the French authorities. On the whole, these supplies were rather meagre, the arms and equipment out-dated. Here, too, I met Captain Antoni Skiba[48], from whom I learned about the final days of the action carried out by the Wołyń Brigade and the 19th Lancers Regiment. Captain Skiba informed me that two columns had

---

47 There was a mustering point in Bessières. Officers who had not been given secondments were directed to one of the Reserves Training Centres in Les Sables-d'Olonne, Fontenay-le-Comte, Niort, Ancenis, Thouars, Luçon, Sables d'Or, Val-André, La Roche-sur-Yon, Bressuire, St. Méen-le-Grand, Loudéac, Châteaubriant, Vichy, Champdeniers, Sept-Fons and Montauban (W. Biegański, *Wojsko Polskie we Francji 1939–1940 [Polish Army in France 1939-1940]*, Warsaw 1967, pg. 156). In actual fact, there was no Podolski Cavalry Brigade or 9th Lancers Regiment Reserves Centre in Sables d'Or.

48 Antoni Skiba (1900–1997) – Lieutenant, regular cavalry officer from September 1926. In 1932, assigned to 11th Lancers Regiment. Awarded the Virtuti Militari Order, V Class, the Cross of Independence and the Cross of Valour. Promoted to Cavalry Captain in 1936. According to OdB on 23 March 1939, Commander of the 2nd Squadron in the 11th Lancers Regiment. In September 1939, with the rank of Cavalry Captain, commanded the 1st Squadron of the 19th Wołyń Lancers Regiment (named after Gen. Edmund Różycki). In 1940, reached France and later Great Britain where – until 1947 – he served successively in: the 24th Lancers Regiment, the 10th Dragoon Regiment, and the Anti-tank Artillery Regiment (units of Gen. Stanisław Maczek's 1st Armoured Division, formed in February 1942). After the war, he settled in London. During the period 1955-56, he held a grant in a School of International Trade. Until 1974, an employee of Alliance Shipping Assurance. In 1971, his book entitled *Boje 19 Pułku Ułanów Wołyńskich w Kampanii Wrześniowej [The Battles of the 19th Wołyń Lancers Regiment in the September Campaign]* was published by the *Przegląd Kawalerii i Broni Pancernej* [Cavalry and Armoured Forces Review]. He died in the Castlethorpe Nursing Home. His ashes were laid to rest in the Columbarium of St. Andrzej Bobola Church in London.

been formed from what remained of the Brigades fighting to the north of Warsaw and these had taken two different routes towards the south and the border. One group, under the command of General Anders[49], the other commanded by Colonel Karcz.[50] Colonel Karcz's group happened on an armoured German unit whose commander advised surrender. Not having any alternative, Colonel Karcz agreed and then spent five years as a German POW.[51]

Captain Skiba was in the rear guard of General Anders's column. One day they came across a German unit whose commander advised General Anders that he should surrender but the General refused. He said he wanted to continue his march towards the Hungarian border and the Germans let him go. A day or two later Anders's column encountered a Bolshevik unit – this time there was no choice, everyone was taken prisoner.[52] When Captain Skiba found out, he decided to disband the rear guard and to go into hiding. One day, a passer-by said to him: "For heaven's sake man, find a barber and get a shave – you're meant to be in hiding but your appearance clearly shows who you are."

During that period in Sables d'Or there was a somewhat strained atmosphere between us. I am sorry that I did not tell Captain Skiba exactly how I had lost contact with the Regiment. I did not have another occasion to speak with him because shortly after that conversation he was moved to another group. I lost

---

49 Władysław Anders (1892–1970) – Major General with seniority as of 1 January 1934. In September 1939, Commander of the Nowogródzka Cavalry Brigade. Commander-in-Chief of the Polish Army in the East and the II Corps, which he commanded during the Battle of Monte Cassino. Died in London and, in accordance with his Will, was buried among his soldiers in the Polish Military Cemetery in Monte Cassino, Italy.

50 Jan Karcz (1892–1943) – Colonel with seniority as of 1 January 1931. Awarded the Virtuti Militari Order, V Class, the Polonia Restituta Order IV Class, the Cross of Valour (4 times) and the Gold Cross of Merit. In 1932, Head of the Department of the Cavalry. In September 1939, he commanded the Mazowiecka Cavalry Brigade. Murdered in Auschwitz concentration camp. Posthumously promoted to the rank of Major-General.

51 In actual fact, during the occupation, Col. Jan Karcz joined the underground resistance in the secret White Eagle Organisation, which was active in the Kraków area. With it, he went on to join the Association of Armed Struggle (ZWZ). At the beginning of 1941, he was arrested by chance during a street round-up in Tarnów. Imprisoned in Lublin Castle on 27 November and transported to the Auschwitz-Birkenau concentration camp as a political prisoner. He joined the secret ZOW, or Military Organisation Union, set up within the concentration camp by Captain Witold Pilecki. In December 1941, most probably betrayed to the camp Gestapo by a traitor. Following brutal interrogation in the bunker of Block 11, moved to the penal company and sent to the camp in Birkenau. There, he set up a branch of the ZOW and commanded it until January 1943. On 23 January, once again moved to the bunker in Block 11 and on 25 January executed at the infamous Black Wall. His body was burned in the crematorium (Note: A.Ś.-J.).

52 Compare: W. Anders, *Bez ostatniego rozdziału. Wspomnienia z lat 1939–1946* [*Without the Final Chapter. 1939-1945 Remembered*], London 1989; S. Koszutski, *Wspomnienia z różnych pobojowisk* [*Recollections from various fields of battle*], London 1972; L. Schweizer, *Wojna bez legendy* [*War without a Legend*], Kirkcaldy 1943; Z.S. Siemaszko, *Generał Anders w latach 1892–1942* [*Gen. Anders during the period 1892-1942*], London – Warsaw 2012.

contact with him and did not meet up again until much later.

I cannot remember how long we stayed in Sables d'Or. We were transferred for further re-organisation to three places in north-eastern Brittany (La Croix, Ploërmel and Talbot). Here, we were once again organised and re-organised. The Reconnaissance Unit of the 3rd Infantry Division comprised a cavalry squadron (six horses had been sent from Coëtquidan), a motorised squadron (carriers), a machine-gun squadron and a supplies unit which included the commander's party.

Personnel included (as far as I recall): Commander – Major Włodzimierz Łączyński[53], 1) Cavalry Squadron – Captain Skupiński[54], 2) Machine-gun Squadron – Captain Mińkowski[55], 3) Motorised Squadron – Captain Strzałkowski[56], Supplies Platoon and Commander's party – a second lieutenant in the Reserves (I do not remember his name).

The *Ordre de Bataille* kept changing as new conscripts arrived – most of them residents of France. Virtually the whole of the reserve Podolska Brigade

---

53 Włodzimierz Hipolit Łączyński (1898–1944) – Cavalry Captain from 1924. In 1932, seconded to service in the 8th Lancers Regiment. Awarded the Silver Cross of Merit. Cavalry Major with seniority as of 1 January 1934. According to OdB on 23 March 1939, Quartermaster (seconded to the 10th Lancers Regiment). In September 1939, Second-in-Command of the 2nd Horse Rifles Regiment, later Commander of the Reconnaissance Unit of the 3rd Infantry Division in France. Killed in 1944 when an allied bomb was dropped by mistake on German POW camp Oflag VI B Dössel.

54 Stefan Bronisław Skupiński (1895–1997) – began military service in 1915 in Gen. Józef Dowbor-Muśnicki's I Corps. Cavalry Captain from 1928. In 1932, seconded to the 16th Lancers Regiment. Next, transferred from Cavalry Officer Corps to Administrative Officer Corps. According to OdB on 23 March 1939, Regional Commander of Military Cavalry Training (seconded to 8th Horse Rifles Regiment). In September 1939, sustained a head wound. Evacuated to Romania and then managed to reach France. After the Fall of France, evacuated to Great Britain. From 26 April 1944, at the disposal of the Special Department of the Staff of the Supreme Commander (previously sworn in as a soldier of the AK Underground Resistance Army, code-name "Totul", however, not sent out to Poland). Awarded the Gold Cross of Merit, the Silver Cross of Merit with Swords, Silver Cross of Merit and the French Croix de Guerre. Lt. Colonel of Cavalry, famed rider and member of the pre-war Polish Olympic team. Buried in America's Częstochowa in Pennsylvania.

55 Michał Mińkowski (1902–1982) – Lieutenant in Regular Cavalry Officer Corps from 1929. In 1932, seconded to the 12th Lancers Regiment. Cavalry Captain from 1937. According to OdB on 23 March 1939, Commander of 1st Platoon, 2nd Training Squadron, seconded to Cavalry Training Centre (Cavalry Officer Cadet School) in Grudziądz. According to personnel records of the Secretarial Office of Regimental Clubs (12th Podolski Lancers Regiment) in September 1939, Mińkowski was Commander of a squadron in the 12th Lancers Regiment. Took part in the French Campaign; from 21 July 1940 to 2 May 1945, POW in German Oflag. During the period 1945–1946, Second-in-Command of the 12th Lancers Regiment. Awarded, among others, the Virtuti Militari Order, the Cross of Valour, the Polonia Restituta Order IV Class and the Gold Cross of Merit. Ashes interred in the Columbarium of the Church of St. Andrzej Bobola in London.

56 Jan Piotr Strzałkowski (1899–1979) – Cavalry Lieutenant from 1922. In 1932, seconded to the 9th Lancers Regiment (delegated to the Cavalry Training Centre in Grudziądz). Cavalry Captain from 1937. According to OdB on 23 March 1939, military dressage course commander – seconded to Cavalry Training Centre (Riding School) in Grudziądz. Died in Liverpool, buried in Bootle Cemetery.

with the officers of the 9th Lancers Regiment found themselves here. It was they who persuaded their eldest member, Captain Hugo Kornberger[57], to add to the official name of the Reconnaissance Unit of the 3rd Division, the words "named after the 9th Małoposki Lancers Regiment" and to try to obtain the agreement of the Supreme Commander, General Sikorski, to this addition.[58] Kornberger did obtain the General's permission and henceforth the Reconnaissance Unit was referred to by that name in all publications.

Among the officers of the 9th Lancers Regiment, the following deserve mention: Captain Kornberger, Lieutenant Wojnarowski[59] and Lieutenant Garapich.[60] In addition there were two of my elder colleagues from Grudziądz: Lieutenant Władysław Piotrowski[61] (from Podhajce) and Lieutenant Stanisław Ruciński[62], as well as Second Lieutenant Michał Zając (graduated 1939) who, as I write these words (July 2011), lives in Australia. Here, too, I came across

---

57 Hugo Henryk Marian de Kornberger (1902–1957) – Cavalry Lieutenant from 1923. In 1932, seconded to 8th Lancers Regiment. Awarded the Cross of Valour. Cavalry Captain from 1937. According to OdB on 23 March 1939, Adjutant and Commander of administrative squadron (officer performing two functions) in the 9th Lancers Regiment. According to personnel records of the 7th Cadre Rifle Brigade dated 21 November 1940, Second-in-Command with the rank of Cavalry Captain of the 7th Anti-tank Company. Died in Dorking (Surrey) and buried there.

58 For more information, see: S. Tomaszewski, *Szkic historyczny 9 Pułku Ułanów Małopolskich [Brief History of the 9th Małopolski Lancers Regiment]*, [in:] *9 Pułk Ułanów Małopolskich [9th Małopolski Lancers Regiment]*, ed. Z. Godyń, Edinburgh 1947, pg. 44–45.

59 Tadeusz Jan Wojnarowski (1907–1961) – 2nd Lieutenant of Cavalry. Lieutenant from 1936. According to OdB on 23 March 1939, seconded to 9th Lancers Regiment ("on the course"). Second-in-Command of the 7th Lubelski Lancers Regiment in the II Corps in Italy. Awarded the Silver Cross of Merit, as well as other Polish and foreign decorations. Died a tragic death in Argentina, buried in the cemetery in Boulogne Sur Mer (a suburb of Buenos Aires).

60 Władysław Michał Józef Garapich (born 1908) – Second Lieutenant of Cavalry from 1930. In 1932, seconded to the 9th Lancers Regiment. Lieutenant from 1933. According to OdB on 23 March 1939, Commander of the 1st Platoon, 4th Training Squadron, Cavalry Reserves Officer Cadet Training School in the Cavalry Training Centre in Grudziądz.

61 Władysław Antoni Junosza-Piotrowski (1911–2001) – graduate of the Cavalry Officer Cadet School in Grudziądz with the rank of 2nd Lieutenant in 1935; Lieutenant from 1939. According to OdB on 23 March 1939, Platoon Commander in the 2nd Squadron of the 9th Lancers Regiment. Remained in Great Britain after the war. For many years, Chairman of the 9th Małopolski Lancers Regimental Association. Awarded the Polonia Restituta Cross (V Class), the Gold Cross of Merit, the Silver Cross of Merit with Swords and British and French decorations. Died in Leicester; his ashes were interred in the family grave in Kraków's Rakowicki Cemetery.

62 Stanisław Feliks Ruciński (1912–2004) – graduate of the Officer Cadet Training School in Grudziądz with the rank of 2nd Lieutenant in 1935; Lieutenant from 1939. According to OdB on 23 March 1939, Platoon Commander in 4th Squadron of the 9th Lancers Regiment. Settled in Scotland after the war and then, in 1988, in Penrhos, North Wales. Buried in Pwllheli Cemetery.

my schoolfriends: Jurek Maramaros[63] and Tadzio Wroński[64], and also Jurek Nawrocki[65] and Tadzio Kasprzycki[66] (the latter from the 14th Lancers Regiment). In April or May, I had a very pleasant surprise when my old groom, Genio Wensak, arrived from internment in Hungary. From then on, he always remained close to me and became my undying friend. We would sometimes be apart for some years only to meet up again.

Reconstruction of the Polish Army and of the political situation continued in France. Generally speaking, one might describe the situation in words borrowed from the First World War: "All quiet on the Western Front". The situation changed suddenly when Hitler breached the neutrality of Holland and Belgium and attacked France. It was then that France's total helplessness was revealed, with its lack of modern tactics and inability to defend its own weakest point – the Belgian-French border. General Sikorski, our Supreme Commander, was particularly shocked as he was totally convinced of France's strength and had, therefore, not prepared a programme of evacuation of the Polish Government and army to Great Britain. The issue of the first 50 visas (later increased to 150) for the Polish Government was a pathetic gesture. A small ship, moored near the Spanish border, was assigned for the purposes of evacuation of the Government. In a book written by a Polish journalist and writer (I do not remember her name) I read that a British soldier used the butt of his rifle to 'help' Mrs Sikorska cross the gangway onto the ship which was standing in the port. The British Ambassador,

---

63 Jerzy Tomasz Maramaros (1913–1992) – officer of the 6th Kaniowski Lancers Regiment, the 5th Armoured Regiment and the 9th Małopolski Lancers Regiment. Awarded the Gold Cross of Merit, as well as Polish, British and French medals. For many years, a member of the Board of the 9th Lancers Regimental Association, and also its Deputy Chairman. Died in London.

64 Tadeusz Romuald Wroński (1918–1994) – officer of the 6th Kaniowski Lancers Regiment and the 9th Małopolski Lancers Regiment. Awarded the Gold Cross of Merit, as well as Polish and British medals. After the war a long-standing member of the Board of the 9th Lancers Regimental Association and its Deputy Chairman. Died in London and buried in Beckenham Cemetery (Kent).

65 Jerzy Tadeusz Nawrocki (1918–2002) – graduate of the Cavalry Officer Cadet School in Grudziądz. Officer in the 14th Jazłowiecki Lancers Regiment. Took part in the Polish September 1939 Campaign, later served with the 1st Armoured Division (1944–1945). Awarded the Cross of Valour, the Gold Cross of Merit, the Silver Cross of Merit with Swords, the Polish Army Medal, the Cross of the 1st Armoured Division, as well as many Polish and foreign awards. Long-standing Chairman of the 14th Jazłowiecki Lancers Regimental Association, Deputy Chairman of the 9th Małopolski Lancers Regimental Association, and member of the Board of the Association of Cavalry Regimental Associations. Died in London, buried in Łańcut.

66 At the end of June 1939, assigned to the 14th Lancers Regiment on a training placement from the Cavalry Officer Cadet Training School in Grudziądz (after completing the first academic year). He figures in the personnel list of the reserves squadron of the 14th Lancers Regiment on 4 September 1939. (2nd Lieut. – regular service). From 14 September in the 2nd Squadron, Marching Regiment of the Podolski Cavalry Brigade, part of which included the 14th Regiment. Figures in the list of members of the 14th Lancers Regiment in France in the period 1939-1940.

who was a frequent guest of General and Mrs Sikorski, watched the incident from the upper deck.

The Polish Army composed of soldiers summoned to France on the order of the Supreme Commander, as well as those who knew nothing of such an order and yet reached France in different ways, risking their lives in the process, had a strength of 80,000 (according to data from the Polish Institute and General Sikorski Museum – PISM). Only 20,000 were evacuated to England. This included the second batch of the Podhalański [Highland] Brigade, sailing from Norway to France which was recalled and re-directed to Great Britain.[67]

Evacuation of the 9th Małopolski Lancers Regiment's Reconnaissance Unit

The order we received read: "Make for the port of St. Nazaire where you will find British ships which will take you to Great Britain." A simple enough order but how do we carry it out? It was impossible to cover a distance similar to that from Warsaw to Kraków in a short period of time and without transport. The German 'Blitzkrieg' had taken everyone by surprise, including all Staff Command and even the Supreme Commander, General Władysław Sikorski, who was apparently travelling round the front in search of French General Weygand, to whom he intended to present some sort of 'plan of salvation'.

In June 1940 (I do not remember the actual date) we were given an order to evacuate which was recalled that same day and repeated on the following day. The following plan was put into action: the unit was split into two parts – the first (armed) unit under the command of Major Łączyński and the second (without armament), under the command of Lieutenant Garapich and his second-in-command, Warrant Officer Michał Zając. Both contingents were to take different routes and head for St. Nazaire under their own steam. British ships would then transport them to Great Britain.

Having sorted out administrative matters, both groups left their positions and marched off southwards in the general direction of the port of St. Nazaire. On the second or third day of their march southwards, Lieutenant Garapich's

---

67   In mid June, the Polish Army in France had a strength of approx. 84,500 troops. After the Fall of France, Polish soldiers made their way to Great Britain either direct from France, or in a roundabout way via Africa and Portugal. According to OdB on 26 June 1940, 1,863 officers and 10,749 land force troops managed to reach Great Britain. These numbers, however, do not include those soldiers who had not yet reached the camps in Britain from their ports of disembarkation. (Z. Wawer, E. Pawlowski, *Polskie Siły Zbrojne na obczyźnie[Polish Armed Forces in Exile]*, [in:] *Wojsko Polskie w II wojnie światowej [The Polish Army in WW2]*, ed. E. Pawlowski, Z. Wawer, Warsaw 2005, pg. 157, 168).

group came across a train standing in a local station. Threatened with force, the reluctant and ill-disposed French train driver agreed to fire up the engine and Lieutenant Garapich's group finally arrived by train at the port of St. Nazaire. The British ships were no longer there. The Lieutenant decided to cross to an island a few miles offshore in fishing boats. They ended up on a nudist beach where they were warmly welcomed by the sunbathers, who offered them tea. On the second or third day, they stopped a passing French collier which took them to Great Britain. I learned of this once both our groups were finally reunited in Great Britain.

After a march lasting several hours, Major Łączyński's group (mine) stopped for an overnight rest. The Major drove off to Divisional Command for a briefing and to find out what was happening. On his return, he told us that the German troops were advancing on Paris at a fast pace and he passed on to the officers an order that the troops conscripted in France be disbanded. I must stress that I have not found any such express order issued by the Supreme Commander in the archives of the Polish Institute and General Sikorski Museum in London.[68] We decided to continue our march. On the second day, now wearied by the march, our drivers began to scour farms along our way searching for means of transport. They eventually found a large coal-fuelled truck (had it been oil powered it would have been useless to us). They managed to get it going and now that we had a means of transport our situation was vastly improved. The truck could take about thirty soldiers, so one-third of our contingent travelled some 15-20 kilometres by truck while the rest marched, then the truck would turn around, pick up the next one third and so on. Two thirds of my group managed to reach St. Nazaire in this manner and there they boarded a British ship in the port and sailed off to Great Britain (Glasgow). When the third group (some 30 Lancers), including myself, arrived in St. Nazaire, there were no longer any ships in the port and the Germans were breathing down our necks. Riding a motorcycle to the port, Major Łączyński got lost and ended up in a POW camp where he died tragically during an American bombing-raid.

Under the circumstances, I took a quick decision. We would cross to an island situated several nautical miles away in fishing boats. And this proved the army adage: "A quick decision, even a bad one, is better than one which takes

---

68 On 18 June 1940, the Polish Ministry of Military Affairs issued a directive allowing commanders to allow a 'quick release' of soldiers who no longer wanted to serve in the army. Almost all the draftees who resided permanently in France took advantage of this opportunity while only a very small number of soldiers who had come from Poland did so. (*ibidem*, pg. 162; PISM, A.IV.8/2, Report by Major-General Marian Kukiel, Libourne, 19 June 1940).

a long time to mature." Remaining on land, we would have been able to reach the unoccupied south of France, while from the island we could well be taken prisoner by the Germans and transferred to one of the POW camps. At that moment, neither option was a surety.

On the second day, a French tanker was passing the island. I sent a Lieutenant of the Reserves (I don't remember his name) by motor-boat, to ask the Captain what his destination was and whether he would agree to take us. It turned out that the tanker was sailing to Great Britain and he agreed to take us with him. The ship was full of oil and sitting so low in the water that when we sat on the deck we had our feet in water. Early in the morning, as we approached the English shore, we heard the roar of engines. We heaved a sigh of relief when a plane with British markings came out of the clouds. We sailed into the port (Falmouth, I think) without any incidents.

When we arrived in Great Britain in June 1940, nobody asked us for visas nor questioned the fact that we were armed. I took note of a big difference between England and France – there was an enormous number of children playing in the street – there were no such scenes in France. In the port, there was a three-wheel, small-engined sports car. Our "experts" were quick to give their opinion: "If they drive cars like that, there's no way they can win the war".

Our unit arrived in England in three groups and having taken various routes. This was due in part to sensible decisions and also to a proverbial stroke of luck. During that initial period after landing in Falmouth, my group changed its quarters in central England several times. The three parts of the unit did not meet up until we were in the Glasgow area in Scotland (I don't remember exactly when that was) and we then continued our reorganisation in south-eastern Scotland. We were first stationed in the town of Dunfermline and quartered in a school where we slept on straw mattresses. My neighbour was a man called Edward Bogusz – a landowner from near Tarnów. After just a few sentences we already knew we had much in common. Edward Bogusz had served with the 2nd Polish Legions' Lancers Regiment and this was a natural link with Rokitna and the famous charge [in 1915]. This unexpected meeting turned into a lifelong friendship which lasted through two generations, including his daughter Jadzia Bajorek and grandson Franuś. And now (2013) there is a third generation, Franuś and Beata's daughter, Natalia.

Tadeusz Bączkowski as a newly commissioned 2nd Lieutenant in
the 19th Lancers Regiment. (Dariusz Szymczyk Collection)

Subalterns of the 19th Lancers Regiment stationed in Ostróg on Poland's eastern border
with the USSR. Lt. Bączkowski is sitting on the left, 1938. (Dariusz Szymczyk Collection)

Sgt. Migdał with "Medzio", the mount ridden by Major Feliks Jaworski, organiser and first commanding officer of the 19th Lancers Regiment. (Dariusz Szymczyk Collection)

Lt. Tadeusz Bączkowski whilst on a short-term commission in the British Army serving in Sierra Leone, West Africa, 1942. (Dariusz Szymczyk Collection)

The Polish 1st Armoured Division in Normandy, early August 1944. The first briefing at Divisional HQ. Seated from the left are: Capt. Leon Czekalski, Maj. Michał Wąsowicz, Anon., Col. Kazimierz Dworak, Maj-Gen. Stanisław Maczek, Maj. Ludwik Stankiewicz, Maj. Stanisław Snarski. Standing from the left are: Lt. Tadeusz Bączkowski, Capt. Tadeusz Wysocki. (Courtesy of the Polish Institute and Sikorski Museum)

The Polish 1st Armoured Division in Normandy, August 1944. Death and destruction during operations leading to the closing of the Falaise Gap at the "Mace" (Chambois). (Courtesy of the Polish Institute and Sikorski Museum)

The Polish 1st Armoured Division in Normandy, August 1944. Death and destruction during operations leading to the closing of the Falaise Gap at the "Mace" (Chambois). (Courtesy of the Polish Institute and Sikorski Museum)

Col. Antoni Grudziński, Deputy Officer Commanding 10th Armoured Cavalry Brigade of the 1st Armoured Division taking the surrender of Wilhelmshaven from the German delegation, May 1945. (Courtesy of the Polish Institute and Sikorski Museum)

Raising the Polish flag at the gates of the German Naval Base in Wilhelmshaven, May 1945. (Courtesy of the Polish Institute and Sikorski Museum)

Tadeusz Bączkowski with his brother, 2nd Lieutenant Jan Bączkowski, in Italy, 1945.
(Dariusz Szymczyk Collection)

The author whilst on a leather crafting course during his service with the
Polish Resettlement Corps, 1948. (Dariusz Szymczyk Collection)

Tadeusz Bączkowski at the printing press of his company "Omega Press", c. 1965.
(Dariusz Szymczyk Collection)

Tadeusz Bączkowski with his wife Janina at the Polish Institute and Sikorski
Museum in London, c. 1980s. (Dariusz Szymczyk Collection)

The Author. (Dariusz Szymczyk Collection)

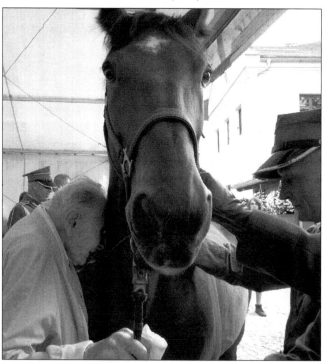

The 99-year old Captain Tadeusz Bączkowski bids an emotional farewell to a horse, during his annual visit to Grudziądz, his old cavalry Alma Mater, August 2013. (Photo: Zofia Majsterek, courtesy of the Foundation for the Preservation of the Polish Cavalry Tradition)

7

1940–1941: Great Britain

In 1940, Gen. Sikorski visited the Polish units. There was a parade and a review. Our unit received a pennant from Sir Patrick Dollan[69] and from then on it always marked the carrier of our Commanding Officer, Colonel Grabowski[70], who had taken it over from Captain Kornberger, when the latter was ill and admitted to hospital. Then, one day, Colonel Grabowski had occasion to cross swords with General Sikorski's daughter during lunch in our mess and a short while later he was transferred and Colonel Eugeniusz (Żenia) Święcicki[71]

---

69 Patrick Joseph Dollan (1885–1963) – Scottish political activist. Worked as a miner. Fought for the rights of workers in Glasgow. During the period 1920–1932, Chairman of the Scottish section of the Independent Labour Party. On expulsion from the party, he formed the Scottish Socialist Party, which was immediately affiliated to the Labour Party. Mayor of Glasgow 1938–1941. "On 31 August 1940, the Reconnaissance Unit celebrated its Regimental Day with great ceremony. That day it received its colours from the City of Glasgow as a symbol of Polish-Scots friendship. The ceremony was attended by the President of the Republic of Poland, Władysław Raczkiewicz, and the Supreme Commander, General Sikorski. During Holy Mass, the Field Bishop of the Polish Army, [Józef] Gawlina, consecrated the Colours, the Mayor of the City of Glasgow, Sir Patric[k] Dollan, and his wife acted as 'god-parents'. After Holy Mass, the ceremony of presentation of the colours took place in the presence of Lord Hamilton, representing His Majesty King George VI." (*9 Pułk Ułanów ... [9th Lancers Regiment ...]*, pg. 49).

70 Ziemowit Grabowski (1898–1985) – Lt. Colonel in the Regular Cavalry Officers' Corps from 1937. According to Polish Army OdB on 1 September 1939, Chief-of-Staff of Command of Cavalry Operational Group no. 1 (unit at the disposal of the Supreme Commander). According to personnel records of the 3rd Infantry Division, prior to its reorganisation into a "light division" (in June 1940), Divisional Chief-of-Staff with the rank of Lt. Colonel. Subsequently in Great Britain. According to personnel records of the 3rd Cadre Rifle Brigade on 1st September 1940, Commander of the 3rd Reconnaissance Unit, and subsequently Second-in-Command of the 2nd Carpathian Rifles Brigade (3rd DSK in the Italian Campaign).

71 Eugeniusz Święcicki (1896–1961) – during the period 1917–1929 in the 1st Krechowiecki Lancers Regiment, first as Platoon Commander, then: Adjutant, Commander of School for Non-Ccommissioned Officers, and Squadron Commander. Next: Quartermaster to the 23rd Lancers Regiment. Held rank of Major from 1929. Awarded the Cross of Valour (three times), the Gold Cross of Merit and the Independence Medal. Promoted to the rank of Lt. Colonel in 1934. According to OdB on 23 March 1939, Second-in-Command of the 4th Lancers Regiment. He went to war as part of the Wilno Cavalry Brigade of Army 'Prusy'. Taken prisoner by the Germans but escaped and made his way to France. In 1940, Commander of the 2nd Wilno Reconnaissance Squadron, the 2nd Infantry Rifles Division with the rank of Lt. Colonel of Cavalry. In Great Britain, according to personnel records of the 1st Rifles Brigade on 1 November 1940, Commander of 1st Reconnaissance Unit of the 1st Rifles Brigade with the rank of Lt. Colonel of Cavalry. According to personnel records of the 7th Infantry Division in 1942, seconded to that Division where, in the rank of Lt. Colonel, he commanded the 7th Reconnaissance Squadron. His three final functions in the Polish Armed Forces during the period 1939–1946 (according to membership records of the "Krechowiak" Secretariate of Unit Clubs): [from] Liaison Officers' section of II Corps in Italy to the 5th Kresowa Infantry Division, Commander of the

took over command.

My friend, Dr Leon Ossowski, suffered some sort of infection in his leg and was hospitalised. When he was able to walk again, he gathered some mushrooms in a wood near the hospital. He brought the mushrooms to the hospital in order to cook them. There was consternation amid the doctors and nurses and they wanted to burn him alive, together with his mushrooms, on account of the "germs" he had brought into the hospital. It was not until some time later that the Poles and Ukrainians taught the locals that forest mushrooms are edible. The forestry authorities found out about Dr Ossowski's expertise. His experience was so valuable to them that they persuaded the Polish authorities to exempt him from military service and subsequently employed him in the Scottish Forestry Commission. Ossowski took over responsibility for the forested areas between Edinburgh and Aberdeen (in 1941, when I was leaving for Africa) and the Galashiels headquarters of the Forestry Commission from its previous Director, a Scotsman. He was quartered in the home of a Mrs McLean. Kathleen, a middle-aged Scots teacher, was also living there and she later became Ossowski's wife.

Shortly after he took over the unit, Colonel Święcicki transferred me, Second Lieutenant Gąska and Lieutenant Stanisław Ruciński to the 4th Reconnaissance Unit in Edzell which was being formed alongside the 4th Infantry Division[72], popularly known as "half-four". Edzell, a lovely, sunny place was located near the eastern shore of the sea which was guarded by the 14th Lancers Regiment. It was they who fished a lifebelt out of the water. It had belonged to the ship "MS Piłsudski", and can now be seen in London, in the Polish Institute and General Sikorski Museum.[73]

In Edzell, I met my Platoon Leader from Grudziądz, Lieutenant Lucjan Pruszyński, Captain Skupiński and other well-known cavalry officers. We were

---

3rd Silesian Lancers Regiment, Second-in-Command of the Wielkopolska Armoured Brigade. Settled in Britain after the war. Worked as a restaurant manager. Died in Brighton and buried in London's Brompton Cemetery.

72 This unit underwent various organisational changes. Formed in August 1940 as the 1st Independent Rifles Brigade, on the orders of the Supreme Commander dated March 1943, renamed the 1st Grenadiers Division then, by order issued in September 1943, changed to the 2nd Grenadiers Division, subsequently by an order dated May 1944 to the Armoured Grenadiers (Cadre) Division and, finally, by order dated February 1945, transformed into the 4th Infantry Division (PISM, A.VI.14/1-18). In actual fact, on 10 December 1940, the author was transferred from the Reconnaissance Unit of the 1st Rifles Brigade to the Reconnaissance Unit of the 7th (Cadre) Rifles Brigade.

73 The lifebelt from MS Piłsudski, which sank off north-eastern England in November 1939, was thrown up by the sea in 1940, on the Barry Links beach in Scotland. This was in the 14th Lancers Regiment's defence sector. At this time, the Regiment formed part of the 10th Armoured Cavalry Brigade (for more information, see: *Dzieje Ułanów Jazłowieckich [History of the Jazłowiecki Lancers]*, collective work, London 1988).

quartered in a large boarding house. Our classes centred on English language lessons. When school was over for the day, the women teachers were glad to give us free lessons. Military subjects were also compulsory. Various classes were organised to fill the programme. Even Scottish dancing was available for those who were interested. "Sikorski's tourists" continued to flood in. We were befriended here by two dogs (every military unit has its share of dog lovers) – a Dalmation and an Alsatian. The Dalmatian somehow took a shine to me. One day its owner telephoned us asking whether her dog was with us. As it happened, I took the call. I informed her that it was and that it had befriended me and that I was wondering how to go about kidnapping it! At that she replied: "No need for kidnapping. It's only a puppy and needs a great deal of exercise which is beyond my means. If you want, you can keep him." And that is how I became the owner of a beautiful Dalmation.

Near Edzell there was a place called Brechin, where the 4th Infantry Division was stationed. It was there that I met Major Adam Będzikowski[74] of the 51st Infantry Regiment from Brzeżany and Captain Brymora[75] of the Border Defence Corps from Ostróg. I visited them quite often.

My transfer to the 4th Reconnaissance Unit was totally groundless, and I could have reported to the Divisional Commander with a complaint, but I

---

74 Adam Będzikowski (born 1896) – Captain of Infantry from 1925. In 1932, seconded to the 51st Infantry Regiment. Next, he was transferred to the Administration Officers' Corps. According to OdB on 23 March 1939, Commander of the Brzeżany National Defence Battalion and Commandant of the 51st Military Training Sector attached to the 51st Infantry Regiment. In September 1939, Commander of the National Defence Battalion forming part of the "Lwów" National Defence Brigade, established in 1936 from reserve and draft troops from the co-called "extra-contingent". In 1940 in France, Administrative Company Commander of the 1st Demi-Brigade, the Independent Highland Rifles Brigade (according to personnel records of the Independent Highland Rifles Brigade on embarkation). Then Paymaster Officer of the 21st (Cadre) Rifles Battalion (according to personnel records of the 4th (Cadre) Rifles Brigade dated 1 September 1940). On 22 December 1942, he figures in the personnel records of the Motorised Infantry Rifles Battalion in Scotland, with the rank of Captain (one of the rifle battalions of the 1st Armoured Division before it was reorganised, set up by order of the Supreme Commander dated 26 February 1942, based on part of the Corps' Heavy Machine Gun Battalions, assigned to the 16th Armoured Brigade and shortly afterwards renamed as 16th Dragoon Battalion, divided into squadrons, so it ceased to be counted as infantry).

75 Bolesław Brymora (1897–1967) – Captain of Infantry from 1930. Awarded the Virtuti Militari Order, V Class, the Cross of Independence, and the Cross of Valour (4 times). In 1932, seconded to the 58th Infantry Regiment. According to OdB on 23 March 1939, Commander of the Military Reserve Company, the "Ostróg" Battalion of the Border Defence Corps. In September 1939, Commander – 5th Company, II Battalion of the 98th (Reserve) Infantry Regiment, later Battalion Commander. According to personnel records of the Independent Highland Rifles Brigade on embarkation in 1940 in France (Adjutant to the Commander of the 1st Battalion, 1st Demi-Brigade). Later Second-in-Command of 3rd Company, 21st (Cadre) Rifles Battalion (data according to personnel records of 4th Cadre Rifle Brigade as of 1 September 1940). On 22 December 1942, he figures in the records of the Motorised Infantry Rifles Battalion in Scotland with the rank of Captain. Died in Wolverhampton.

refrained from making an issue of it since an opportunity had presented itself to serve in the Colonial Service. The British authorities were afraid that, once the Germans had occupied the whole of France, they would also occupy the French colonies in Africa along with the port of Dakar. This would constitute a considerable threat to communication lines in the Atlantic and in the four British colonies in West Africa. To this end, they decided to increase the strength of their military units in the colonies.

Polish officers in the British Colonial Service

In 1941, the British military authorities approached the Polish Government in London, asking for a loan of 500 younger officers to serve in the British Colonies in West Africa. Applications for a two-year contract were supposed to be voluntary. Convinced that, in the situation in which we found ourselves, my absence from the Polish Army would in no way be detrimental to my army career, I applied without further ado. A two-year contract with the full rights of a British officer allowed for an extension of the contract for a further two years.

Shortly after my application, I received confirmation of my acceptance in the rank of Second Lieutenant in the Sierra Leone Regiment of the 2nd Royal West African Frontier Force. I was also given a ticket and an order to report in the transit camp in the Marylebone Hotel in London. Before leaving Edzell, I travelled to Galashiels to leave my dog with some Scottish friends and to bid farewell to my good friend, Leon Ossowski.

At that time, London was being bombed by the Germans. Apart from Polish pilots, Polish anti-aircraft guns were also used to defend London. [Before the war] we had had to sell off eight such guns in order to be left with just one. In London, people took refuge in air-raid shelters and underground passages and slept on Underground Railway platforms. During daytime, they worked to clear rubble from the streets. The King and Queen frequently visited bomb-damaged areas. Otherwise, London functioned as normal; shops and coffee houses were open. Cinemas had just begun to show the film *Gone with the Wind*. Tickets were sold out right up to March 1943.

Apart from me, Jan Kwaśnicki, Mieczysław Przybyś, Stanisław Trybulec and Witold Wróblewski[76] were also seconded to Sierra Leone.

---

76 For more information, see: PISM, A.XII.17/1, List of Polish Officers in West Africa.

Recruitment Course

The British demanded a contingent of five hundred junior officers (Second Lieutenants) for service in the Colonies and this was the number which applied: three hundred and fifty from Great Britain and one hundred and fifty from the Middle East.[77] While waiting for transport (a convoy to Sierra Leone) my group and I were sent off for basic training in necessary drill – all the commands seemed similar to Polish ones but were carried out differently by the British. Not only did we have to learn how to carry out the commands correctly but also how to give commands and instructions, and how to make reports and present dispatches. There were thousands of such tiny regulations, not to mention the correct method of carrying a swagger stick tucked under the arm!

As the schedule for the departure for West Africa kept changing, we were ordered to attend a second such course in a Scots Unit (the 5th Black Watch Battalion) in the north of Scotland. And there, too, the Battalion Sergeant Major trained us in drill and how to issue commands correctly, so that we would not stand out from the British officers. For this reason, our uniforms were devoid of any Polish markings so that the native soldiers would not think that we were somehow different. In the near future, it would transpire that this was a great help to us during the first days of our stay in the 2nd Battalion in Sierra Leone.

---

77 Compare: pg. 24.

8

1941–1943: Royal West African Frontier Forces

When I volunteered to serve in the British Colonial Forces, I was driven by a desire for new experiences, I wanted to get to know another continent and peoples of another race. I assumed that, in the coming two years, nothing would change much on the European continent and that a two-year absence from the Polish Army would not have an adverse effect on my military career. My knowledge of Africa was limited to what I had learnt in school. And anyway, to be honest, I did not remember much from those lessons.

Our strong convoy of destroyers sailed in a roundabout route, zig-zagging among dangerous points known to the British navigation authorities. We arrived safely in the port of Freetown in Sierra Leone. It was in the train, while waiting for the journey to the barracks of the 2nd Battalion in the depths of the hinterland, that I experienced my first disappointment. A passing black Negro stole my pipe which was lying by the open window. The pipe had a sentimental meaning as I had received it from a friend who had been preparing to be parachuted into Poland. During my two years in Africa, I never smoked a pipe. It was not until I was back in London in 1943 that I bought a similar pipe and began to smoke again.

From Freetown, we travelled to the Battalion's summer camp. Individual huts had been built for us out of branches of palm trees and an elephant grass which was reminiscent of our reeds, except that it was grey and burned by the sun. [...] The furnishings consisted of: a camp bed with a mosquito net, a small table, chair and a canvas wash-basin on a stand. There was also an officers' and non-coms' mess in the camp for Europeans, an infirmary and outbuildings. The Battalion consisted of four companies (A, B, C and D) and a Command.

I was assigned a 'boy' for my personal care (the equivalent of a 'batman' in the Polish Army). My 'boy' was about forty years old and had grey glints in his hair. He was well versed in his duties: he cleaned, washed and ironed my khaki drill and kept all my leather items clean as they were easily damaged by damp in that climate. The soldiers themselves also maintained cleanliness – both personal and with regard to their belongings.

I was assigned to A Company in the 1st Platoon. As I stood in front of the platoon I felt a sudden panic "Good Lord, how will I tell them apart?"! All the faces looked the same to me. However, by the second day, I learned that every Negro is different. They have different smiles, they speak differently – they're all individuals, just like Europeans.

As we marched through the bush during our first exercises and the native soldiers often had to cut a path with their machetes, I felt ill at ease. I soon learned that Sierra Leone does not have any wild animals such as lions or tigers – only large, wild monkeys and wildcats which are as afraid of people as we are of them. That is why they live in the deep hinterland, in places which are not easily accessible to people. I never saw any wild monkeys and wildcats – except from a safe distance. On our narrow paths, we could sometimes happen on a snake, lazing in the sun. We counted on the sharp eyes of the native soldiers, hoping they would spot the snakes in time, or that the snakes would be frightened off by our voices.

Mosquitos posed the greatest danger to our health; a mosquito bite could cause malaria. During my two-year service in Sierra Leone, I had malaria twice but thankfully it did not re-occur after my return to Great Britain.

I will not describe the classes and training because these are similar in all armies – although at that time, in the 1940s, the concepts and methods in the British and French armies were more outdated, even in comparison to our – Polish – ideas and methods. Luckily, we never experienced combat in West Africa; the Germans did not attempt to invade French Liberia.

The Negroes, like other southern races, are less immune to cold than Europeans. During the cooler months, they would attend morning drill in winter greatcoats. The extent of English faith in their combat skills is best reflected by the fact that the West African units which were sent to Burma did not take part in action but were employed in carrying ammunition and equipment. Negro non-commissioned officers were a tremendous help in the daily training programme. Their knowledge of English was very good and thus they were better able to explain military concepts to the rank and file troops in their universally understood dialect.

As there were so any tribes and dialects in Sierra Leone, the British taught the locals the basics of the English language. In Nigeria, where one major type of dialect was spoken (*hausa*), English was also taught. And the Englishmen themselves learnt the *hausa* language. This policy, however, proved to be a mistake, along with the arrival of supplementary reserves from England during the war. Thanks to the fact that I and my colleagues spoke reasonably good English, we never experienced any problems with regards to language or nationality. For this reason, I have pleasant recollections of my two-years of service in the British Colonial Forces and in Africa. I treated this period as a valuable life experience. My knowledge of English improved considerably and, to a great degree, this decided on my further career in the Polish Army.

I obtained the relevant documents and in September 1943 I arrived back in Glasgow. Having served two years I took a month's leave, most of which I spent in the north-east of Scotland, between Edinburgh and Aberdeen.

9

1943: Back in Great Britain

After a two-year stay in Africa, in the autumn of 1943 I began my monthly leave in Scotland. I returned to where I belonged on record – to the 4th Reconnaissance Unit in Edzell. There I met up with my colleagues and my Platoon Commander from Grudziądz – Lucjan Pruszyński.

The command of the newly forming 4th Division[78], nicknamed the 'half four', was stationed in Brechin. There, once again, I met Major Adam Będzikowski of the 51st Rifle Regiment from Brzeżany, as well as Captain Brymora of the Border Defence Corps from Ostróg. I spent most of my leave at the home of Leon Ossowski in Galashiels where I had occasion to marvel at the difference between beautiful, lush green Scotland and the grey, sunburnt greenery of Africa. Leon and Kathleen were now married. I also met with Genio Wensak, who had married a Scotswoman in the meantime.

The Reconnaissance Unit named after the 9th Lancers regiment was stationed in a mill in Galashiels, opposite the building where a chiropodist, Miss McLean, practiced. The Lancers would come to her for various chiropody treatments.

The film *Gone with the Wind* was still being shown in London, in the same cinema, but it was impossible to get tickets.

Here, too, a sorry surprise awaited me – my Dalmation went down with canine distemper and unfortunately departed this world.

During my service in Africa in 1942, by order of the Supreme Commander, General Sikorski, issued on 25 February 1942, the 1st Polish Armoured Division began to form in the south-east of Scotland. General Stanisław Maczek[79] became its commanding officer. The Division's Staff was located in Peebles. Having given some thought to my further active service, I decided to report to the Division's Commander in the hope that I might get a long-term secondment to a permanent unit. As I waited to be seen by the Chief-of-Staff, Colonel Stankiewicz[80], I met

---

78 Compare footnote 72.
79 Stanisław Władysław Maczek (1892–1994) – Commander of the 1st Armoured Division and its preceding units: the 10th Motorised Cavalry Brigade and the 10th Armoured Cavalry Brigade. Promoted to the rank of General in 1990. After the war, he settled in Edinburgh. He was buried among his soldiers in the Polish Military Cemetery in Breda, in Holland.
80 At the time described by the author, Ludwik Antoni Stankiewicz was still a Major. He was promoted

Colonel Zgorzelski.[81] He was surprised to see me there. I told him that I had just returned from Africa and was looking for a new secondment. He answered: "Join me in the Dragoons, then". I had friends and colleagues in the Dragoons, so the proposition was appealing.

At the meeting with the Chief-of-Staff, I told him about my 2-year service with the British Army in West Africa. At that, Colonel Stankiewicz stated that he had an immediate need for two liaison officers with a good knowledge of English. He kept me on as a liaison officer in the Division's Staff and, having completed all the necessary formalities, I was seconded to the Administrative Squadron of the 1st Armoured Division. After that, Major Kamil Czarnecki[82], Staff First Officer, acquainted me with my duties.

I was to maintain contact with the Regimental Commanders, to whom I travelled with orders or reports on the current situation from General Maczek, and vice-versa. I was assigned a small armoured scout car with a driver. On one occasion during hostilities, Divisional Staff Command stopped for the night and was bombed by the American air force. That night I had slept by my scout car and it was not until morning that I found out about the bombing. Colonel Żebrowski's[83] command vehicle was also bombed; Colonel Żebrowski was

---

to Lt. Colonel in recognition of his outstanding services in combat in Normandy (particularly in the Chambois region).

81 Władysław Zgorzelski (1901–1998) – Cavalry Captain in 1932. In 1932, seconded to the 15th Lancers Regiment. Awarded the Virtuti Militari Order, the Cross of Valour, the Independence Medal and the Silver Cross of Merit. According to OdB on 23 March 1939, Commander of the 4th Company, 4th Horse Rifles Regiment. In September 1939, second operational officer in the Command of the Nowogrodzka Cavalry Brigade. Subsequently taken prisoner by the Soviets but managed to escape. On reaching France, he was assigned to the 10th Armoured Cavalry Brigade. After the fall of France, he found himself in Great Britain, where he was given command of the 14th Lancers Regiment. Next, Commander of the 10th Dragoon Regiment in Gen. Stanisław Maczek's 1st Armoured Division. On 9 September 1944, sustained heavy wounds in Belgium. After the war, settled in Edinburgh. Prior to the Second World War, twice Polish Army equestrian champion and once runner-up. After the war, trained equestrian teams in various countries (Great Britain, Ireland, USA, Mexico, Chile, Argentina, Peru and Uruguay). The International Federation for Equestrian Sports awarded him the 'Ordre de Honor Equestre Internationale'. He died in Edinburgh.

82 Kamil Bogumił Czarnecki (1912–2001) – Lieutenant Regular Cavalry Officers' Corps from 1937. According to OdB on 23 March 1939, seconded to City of Warsaw Command. Studied at the Technical University of Warsaw. After September 1939, interned in Romania. Reached France, where he joined the 10th Armoured Cavalry Brigade. Once in Great Britain – according to membership records of the Office of Unit Associations – in 1943, Liaison Officer in the 1st Armoured Division, in 1944 – Operational Officer of the 1st Armoured Division and in the perod 1945-47, officer of the Operational Department in General Staff in London. After the war, he settled permanently in London.

83 Marian Włodzimierz Żebrowski (1896–1992) – Lieutenant in Regular Cavalry Officers' Corps from 1922. In 1932, seconded to the 4th Armoured Squadron. According to OdB on 23 March 1939, with the rank of Captain (from 1934) seconded to Ministry of Military Affairs Armoured Forces Command as head of training department. In the Polish Army from 1 November 1918. Took part in the September 1939 Campaign and in the French Campaign. From January 1944, head of supplies in

wounded and sent back to Edinburgh. While still under treatment he was involved in a car accident, and then developed tetanus. He lay unconscious in hospital for seven months. During a break in action, I was sent to Edinburgh for an examination at the Military Academy. I took the opportunity to visit Colonel Żebrowski in hospital – he was still unconscious. I did not pass the examination – I had not been able to prepare for it. I returned to my duties in Divisional Staff Command.[84]

the 1st Armoured Division. Awarded the Cross of Valour (4 times), the Silver Cross of Merit and the Croix de Guerre. Co-founder and first editor of the *Cavalry and Armoured Forces Review*. Polish Army Colonel and historian, died in Warsaw. In accordance with his Will, an urn with part of his ashes was interred in his parents' grave in Puławy, and another in his family grave in Streatham Park Cemetery in London.

84 The author returned to the 1st Armoured Division on 2 January 1945. He continued to hold the position of Liaison Officer. The Service Record File confirms the information that he was sent to the Military Academy.

10

1944: The March on Berlin

In 1944, we moved to central England, where reorganisation and training continued in preparation for the Normandy landings. At the end of July, we landed in Normandy together with the Canadian Army. I remember the painful sight which faced us – the bombed terrain along a canal defended by German troops. All around was wrecked equipment of various types, and the bodies of dead soldiers and horses. I never imagined that the Germans had so many horses in their foremost defence lines. The first town in which the Division halted was Caen. There, General Maczek called a briefing of all the highest commanding officers and informed them of the task awaiting the Division.[85]

From Caen, the Division set out on its victorious march through France, Belgium, Holland and Germany which ended in May 1945 with the German surrender in Wilhelmshaven. On one of the German ships in Wilhelmshaven, we discovered a brass eagle which had been removed from the building of Polish Fleet Command in Oksywa [Gdynia] (it can be seen now in the Polish Institute and General Sikorski Museum in London).

Then came the start of the occupation of the northern region of Germany by the 1st Armoured Division, which had captured it. Divisional Staff Command was located in Meppen. For the next two years, under the command of General Klemens Rudnicki[86], the Division carried out occupation duties in the north-eastern areas of Germany.

I recall the entire period of the Division's combat trail, from Caen to Wilhelmshaven and the occupation, with great pleasure. I consider it to have been a great honour to serve in such an élite formation as the 1st Polish Armoured Division. I was on friendly terms with the other officers in Staff Command, and with the higher commands of both Brigades and with the Regimental commanders,

---

85 J.L. Englert, K. Barbarski, *Generał Maczek i żołnierze 1 Dywizji Pancernej [Gen. Maczek and the Soldiers of the 1st Armoured Division]*, London 1992, pg. 70.
86 Klemens Stanisław Rudnicki (1897–1992) – in September 1939, Commander of the 9th "Lwów" Infantry Division, formed in the first days of 1941 in Totskoye, near Tchkalov in Soviet Russia. According to 5th Kresowa Infantry Division's OdB on start of action on 21 March 1944, Second-in-Command of the Division, with the rank of Colonel of Cavalry. Fought at Monte Cassino and Bologna. From May 1945, Commander of the 1st Armoured Division (succeeding General Stanisław Maczek). Settled in London after the war. Promoted to the rank of Lieutenant-General in 1990.

whom I met during official briefings and in various other circumstances.

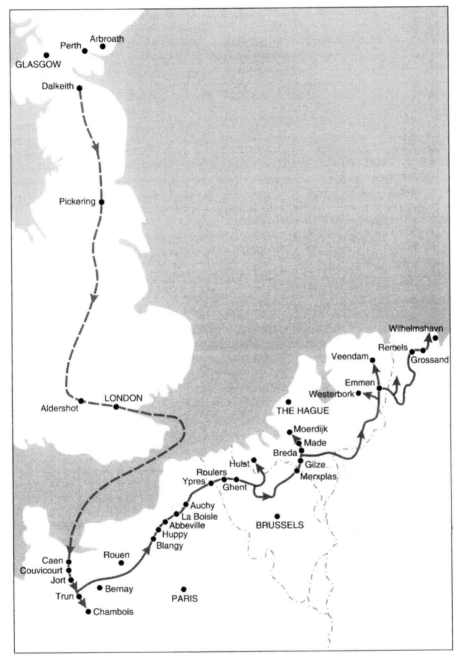

Route of the Polish 1st Armoured Division in the North-West Europe Campaign 1944-1945 (by kind permission of Evan McGilvray, *Man of Steel and Honour: General Stanisław Maczek,* Helion and Company Ltd., Solihull 2012, p.135).

11
1945: The end of hostilities

Shortly after hostilities had ceased in 1945 and after the signing of an agreement [*sic*!] regarding the occupation of the north-[eastern] region of Germany by the 1st Armoured Division, I was sent to Denmark in order to bring Admiral Unrug's[87] wife and son from Copenhagen to Meppen. I have no idea why the Admiral's son did not have the relevant documents; nonetheless, we managed to cross the border without incident.[88] At that time, controls on the border were not too strict and I managed to deal with the situation with the help of Consular officials.

Taking advantage of the fact that nothing of import was happening at the time, I decided to search for my elder brother, Kazimierz[89], an officer of the 14th Infantry Regiment who had been wounded in September 1939 and had spent five years as a German POW. In 1939, his prisoner-of-war camp (I do not remember what it was called) was somewhere close to the Polish border. During hostilities and the encroachment of the Russian armies, the Germans evacuated this camp westwards. I found my brother in Germany – I don't recall where exactly – and brought him to Meppen.

I was on friendly terms with Colonel Dec[90], Commander of the 3rd [Rifle]

---

87 Józef Michał Hubert Unrug (1884–1973) – graduate of high school in Dresden and Naval Academy. During the period 1904–1918 he served in the German Navy. When Poland regained independence, Captain of the Polish Navy from 1924. From 1925, Admiral of the Fleet. Promoted to the rank of Rear Admiral in 1933. In September and October 1939, fought in the defence of the Hel Peninsula, from October 1939 to May 1945 prisoner in various German POW camps. During the period 1945–1947 First Deputy Head of the HQ of the Polish Navy in London. In 1948, settled in Agadir (French Morocco). Vice Admiral as of 2 September 1946. Awarded the Polonia Restituta Order (IV and III Class), the Virtuti Militari Order IV Class, the Gold Cross of Merit and many other Polish and foreign decorations. He died in Lailly-en-Val in France.

88 According to the author's explanations, he was transported in a car boot.

89 Kazimierz Bączkowski (1910–1972) – Lieutenant in Infantry Officer Corps from 1937. According to OdB on 23 March 1939, Liaison Platoon Commander, seconded to the 14th Infantry Regiment. According to personnel records of the 14th Ziemia Kujawska Infantry Regiment dated 1 September 1939, Liaison Officer with the rank of Lieutenant. Wounded on 18 September (in Budy Stare). According to membership records of the Office of Unit Associations (Podhalański Rifles Squadron, the 1st Armoured Division), his last three positions during the period 1939–1945 were: Liaison Officer in 14th Infantry Regiment (1939), German prisoner-of-war (1939–1945), Company Commander in Podhalański Rifles Squadron (1945–1947). Died in Hove.

90 Władysław Dec (1998–1965) – Regular Infantry Captain from 1928. Awarded the Virtuti Militari Order (V Class), the Silver Cross of Merit and the Independence Medal. In 1932 seconded to the 81st

Brigade, so I had no problem in arranging for my brother to be assigned to the 'Podhalan' [Highlanders] Battalion, where he was given the position of Platoon Commander. Later he would be transferred to Great Britain along with the Division. After being demobbed, he lived and worked in London. He died in 1972 and was buried in South Ealing Cemetery.

In 1945, Platoon Leader Jan Szlachetko[91] arrived from Italy. He brought with him a large truckful of gifts for Poles who had been deported from Poland to Germany as forced labour. Given the opportunity, I took a short leave and travelled in the same truck to Italy to meet with my younger brother, Jan[92], who was serving in the II Corps. Together, we toured round the monuments of the Eternal City which was of special significance, particularly for us Poles.

Before the war, Janek had been a law student. After the outbreak of the Second World War, whilst he was crossing the border with Romania, he was captured by the Bolsheviks and deported to Russia. Following the Sikorski–Majski Pact[93] he managed to join General Anders's II Corps and was evacuated from Russia with the Corps.[94] He took part in the battles of the Italian Campaign and was assigned to a military police unit. Together with the II Corps, he then moved to Great Britain and, after demobilisation, settled in London where he later died

Infantry Regiment, which was commanded at that time by Col. Stanisław Maczek. Promoted to the rank of Major in 1936. According to OdB on 23 March 1939, Department Head, with secondment to General Command Department of the Ministry of Military Affairs. In September 1939, Quartermaster (in the rank of Major) of the "Stryj" Group, formed on 10/11 September 1939 and tasked with defence of lines of communication with Romania. In view of the invasion of Poland by Soviet forces, the Group was given orders to cross the border to Hungary or Romania (carried out on 18–21 September). In 1940, in France, as Commander of the II Battalion of the 1st Demibrigade, the Independent Podhalański Rifles Brigade, with the rank of Lt. Colonel. Then, in Great Britain as Commander of the Podhalański Rifles Battalion, forming part of the 3rd Rifles Brigade, set up in 1943 as a result of the reorganisation of the 1st Armoured Division. According to personnel records of the 3rd Rifles Brigade, Second-in-Command of the Brigade at start of action. From 16 January 1945, Commander of the 3rd Rifles Brigade. Died in Warsaw and buried in the Military Cemetery.

91 Jan Szlachetko (1909–1975) – soldier of the Independent Carpathian Rifles Brigade; took part in the Battles for Tobruk and in action in the Tobruk area. After the war, active in ex-combatant and educational matters. Died in London and buried in South Ealing Cemetery.

92 Jan Bączkowski (1915–1964) – according to application for membership of the Association of Polish Economists and Lawyers in Italy, dated 1 July 1946, in 1938 he graduated from the Jan Kazimierz University in Lwów with the degree of Master of Law. Seconded with the rank of 2nd Lieutenant to the 22nd Artillery Supplies Company in the II Corps in Italy. Died in London.

93 The Sikorski-Majski Pact of 30 July 1941 reinstated diplomatic relations between Poland and the USSR which had been broken off on 17 September 1939 following the Soviet invasion of Poland. The Pact was signed in London by the Premier of the Polish Government, Gen. Władysław Sikorski and the Ambassador of the USSR, Ivan Majski. The President of the Republic of Poland, Władysław Raczkiewicz, did not counter-sign the Pact, and it retained the form of an ordinary protocol.

94 Author's mental shortcut. Jan Bączkowski joined the Polish Armed Forces in the USSR (set up on the strength of the Sikorski-Majski Pact). The II Corps was not formed until the summer of 1943 in the Middle East.

and was also buried in Ealing.

12

1946

In 1946 (I do not remember the actual date), I was sent with Major Pieregorodzki[95] to Dover to supervise the arrival of units of the II Corps by rail transport and to arrange for their onward journeys to suitable locations within Great Britain. We were assisted by 10-12 rank and file soldiers from our Unit which had arrived in Great Britain earlier. Among them was Leszek Wróblewski[96] of the [10th] Hussar Regiment. He stood out from his companions in his bearing, his intelligence and I frequently assigned him to special tasks.

We were quartered in barracks. From there we descended to the port down winding steps hewn out of the rock by French prisoners during the Napoleonic Wars. When we had a free moment, we would go to a pub for a drink. There I met a British officer who acted as a liaison between us and the railway authorities. Whilst in Scotland, I had learned to drink whisky with water but from the moment I tried the dark coloured Captain Morgan rum with Coca-Cola, I lost my 'loyalty' to whisky and favoured my newly acquired taste.

Our work in Dover consisted of disembarking the units from their ship and transferring them to a set of railway wagons which was waiting on a platform, and then sending them off to their new locations in Scotland. Luckily, there were no serious accidents during the transfer from ship to the railway carriages.

At this time, I was responsible for a large, black Labrador, called Reks. One day, I had to go aboard a newly arrived ship and I put Leszek in charge of the dog. Reks had a loose dog collar and when he failed to see me anywhere nearby, he became uneasy, slipped off the dog collar and dashed off to find me. He rushed onto a platform but, not seeing me there, began to run through the railway tunnel which ended in a station in the town. It is difficult to describe what we

---

95 Anatol Pieregorodzki (1906–1962) – Cavalry Officers' Corps – Lieutenant from 1932. In 1932, seconded to the 10th Lancers Regiment. Promoted to the rank of Captain in 1939. According to OdB on 23 March 1939, Commander of Traffic Regulation Platoon assigned to the 10th Motorised Cavalry Brigade. Crossed into Hungary together with the Brigade. Served in Gen. Maczek's 1st Armoured Division. Died in Toronto, Canada and buried there.

96 Lesław Antoni Wróblewski (1927–2012) – in April 1940, deported by the Soviets to Kazachstan, together with his family. Followed the Polish Army's trail through the Middle East, Palestine and Italy, reaching Great Britain in 1946. After demobilisation, worked as a tour guide in Europe and subsequently continued to work in the tourist industry until his retirement. Died in London.

went through. At any moment, Reks could have been electrocuted (we did not know whether the current was on, or not). When, back in the barracks, we saw a happy Reks wagging his tail, our joy was boundless. I will never find out how Reks managed to find his way back to the barracks. To tell the truth, he did often ride with me by car from the barracks to the town, to a café, or to meet friends but how he actually found his way from the town to the barracks will forever remain a mystery.

Our mission in Dover accomplished, I returned with Major Pieregorodzki to Divisional Staff[97]; meanwhile, the Lancers who had been assisting us returned to their own units and I lost contact with Leszek. I know that he worked for some time in a hotel in Folkestone. It was not until many years later, in London, after a Mass in the [Polish] Church of St. Andrzej Bobola, that an elderly grey-haired man with a paunch approached me. Seeing the confusion on my face, he introduced himself as Leszek Wróblewski. And then I recalled the handsome young Hussar from Dover.

From then on, we regularly met in POSK – the Polish Social and Cultural Centre.[98] Leszek would call for me every Saturday and take me to the Club, and then drive me home. It was then that I learnt of his many experiences, both those from the period of deportation to Russia, as well as his later experiences as an émigré. I found out that at one point he had been a manager in the "Sirocco" coffee bar in [London's] High Street Kensington. I had passed that coffee bar so many times and was often tempted to go in for a coffee but somehow, I never did. A pity, as then we would have met much earlier. He later worked in a Travel Agency, together with General Rudnicki who was apparently very well disposed towards him. My acquaintance with Leszek started in Dover, in 1946, and subsequently

---

97 Captain-of-Horse Tadeusz Bączkowski was temporarily assigned to the Port of Dover Liaison Section from 14 August to 31 December 1946, which was then extended to 31 March 1947; on 5 April, he joined the ranks of the Polish Resettlement Corps, which he left on 4 April 1949, and transferred to civilian life.

98 The Polish Social and Cultural Association (POSK) in London – the initial concept was presented on 15 February 1964 at a General Meeting of the Federation of Poles in Great Britain. It was to be a Registered Charity, under British law. Founded on 23 July 1964. The first Annual General Meeting took place on 17 February 1966, with the participation of 122 people. With proxy votes this amounted to 365 votes out of a total of 472. On 6 March 1971, Bishop Władysław Rubin consecrated the foundation stone of the future POSK building, in the presence of Polish organisations from around the world. The official opening took place in 1974. Almost all cultural and social organisations found a home for themselves in the new building. The Polish Library and the Polish University Abroad were transferred to POSK. POSK became the heart of the Polish community in London; it housed clubs, coffee bars, restaurants and a theatre. Tadeusz Bączkowski recalled: "The émigré community built a splendid edifice out of voluntary contributions, which to this day houses the Polish Cultural and Social Centre. All our Polish organisations hold meetings there, plays are performed in the theatre, and various ceremonies and National events take place there."

grew into a rapport and friendship which lasted until his death in 2012.

13

1947–1950: Learning to live in exile

B y 1947, enormous political changes had taken place in Poland. The [Communist] Interim Lublin Committee was transformed into a "Polish Government" which was recognised by all European countries, including Great Britain. In view of this, the British government had to revoke its recognition of the Polish Government-in-Exile in London and, consequently, disbanded the Polish Army.[99] This meant that we were suddenly no longer soldiers but a civilian community. We were issued with special identification papers and the British government gave us three alternatives: return to Poland, life in exile or domicile in Great Britain. I chose the third option.

For those who decided to remain in Great Britain, a Polish Resettlement Corps was set up to prepare us for civilian life. Various training programmes were organised for the soldiers in a variety of different trades, e.g. shoe-maker, tailor, barber, carpenter etc.

I chose a course in the production of leather goods. For my diploma project, I made a leather camera case. After completing the course, I immediately found work in a factory producing women's handbags. The factory was located in the London district of Stoke Newington and I moved there. During the first few days after moving, I met up with two former colleagues from Brzeżany: Bronek and Ludwik Pawluk. They ran a stationery shop (mostly selling newspapers and cigarettes), which they leased from a wholesaler. They persuaded me and my elder brother, Kazik, to rent a 'stationer's shop' from the same wholesaler. They would try to ensure that he supplied us on favourable terms. We agreed and during a meeting with the wholesaler we agreed to rent a building from him at 128

---

99 In Moscow, on 21 July 1944, a Polish Committee of National Liberation was established. The following day, its political manifesto was made public (the July Manifesto, or PKWN Manifesto). On 31 December of the same year, the State National Council decided to transform the Polish Committee of National Liberation into an Interim Government. On 28 June 1946, the Interim Government of National Unity (TRJN) was established. Barely a few days later, on 5 July, Great Britain, the United States of America and other states revoked their recognition of the Polish Government in London and gave their approval to the Interim Government of National Unity. On 30 June 1946, a people's referendum took place (on the strength of an Act of the State National Council – KRN). On 19 January 1947, elections to the Sejm (Poland's Lower House of Parliament) took place, nicknamed the Miracle of the Ballot Box. Like the previous results of the people's referendum, these results, too, were falsified.

Kingsland Road. He was to supply us with goods on a *sale or return* basis. They were really very good terms, a rare proposal from a wholesaler.

In 1948, we registered the shop under the trading name "Lech & Brothers" (the English pronounced the name Lech [Leh] as 'Letch'). Kazik ran the shop and I continued to work in the handbag factory, while occasionally collecting goods, or delivering orders. In order to be able to help my brother during the daytime, I changed my daytime job in the women's handbag factory for night shifts in a factory producing car parts (the CAV Company). My work involved hand grinding of pistons for Diesel engine fuel injection pumps. This enabled me to spend a few daytime hours in transporting supplies for the shop and delivering orders.

In 1950, a one-year course was established in foreign trading. I decided to apply for it and was accepted. I also persuaded Janusz Ossowski (the brother of my friend from the Battle of Mokra, Leon Ossowski) to take up the course as he was then working as a miner. Completion of this course opened up opportunities to apply for office work. Having completed the course, I was employed by the Millman Brothers import company in East London. We imported clocks from the Black Forest (Germany)[100] and Switzerland (cuckoo clocks). I do not know why I changed my job in Millman Brothers for a job in the Sevel & Crowther Company, which imported carpets.

During this period, we were approached by a young Englishman who proposed that we purchase a small hand-operated printing press. He said he would teach me to print and would introduce me to his clients. One day he arrived with a small hand machine and moveable type, and various brochures. Unfortunately, once he had received the money – and it was quite a considerable sum – we never saw him again. I was left to my own devices with all the bits and pieces. I had to persevere and to decipher the brochures, learn type-setting and printing on my own. All this time, I continued to work at night. I printed visiting cards and invitations. With time, news of my activities spread throughout the Polish community and Polish organisations and this, in turn, led to further events …

---

100 The author is doubtless thinking of so-called 'Schwartzwalders', or cuckoo clocks, for which the German Schwarzwald (Black Forest) is famed." (note: A.Ś.-J.).

14

1955–1988

In 1955, two Navy officers approached us: Captain Busiakiewicz[101] and Captain Wroński[102] with a proposal that we buy the "Omega Press" for one thousand pounds. It belonged to a young Pole who was emigrating to Canada. After some consideration, we agreed to buy the printworks and we signed a contract with the two Captains: Captain Busiakiewicz was to provide orders for printing and Captain Wroński was to run the office (book-keeping and tax returns), while I was to deal with the printing. We worked as a team for two years. The conditions were unfavourable for me as, in order to deal with the orders, I had to work overtime. Without overtime, I would not be able to fulfil the orders but, by paying myself for the overtime, I was considerably reducing the sum of money which was to be divided between us. So, I put a proposal to our partners, that we should dissolve the partnership, and they agreed. We remained in constant touch and friendship. They continued to supply me with orders, which I carried out for them, at special trading prices. I last saw Captain Busiakiewicz when he was 103 years old and resided in the Polish 'Antokol' Residential Care Home, near

---

101 Jan Feliks Busiakiewicz (1907–2010) – 2nd Lieutenant in the Navy from 1930. In 1932, seconded to Fleet and Sub-unit Command in Gdynia. Promoted to the rank of Lieutenant Commander in 1938. According to OdB on 23 March 1939, Second-in-Command of the 2nd Naval Anti-aircraft Artillery Squadron. Following the capitulation of the Hel peninsula, prisoner-of-war from 2 October in POW camp in Woldenberg, then from February 1945 in Sachsenhausen Concentration Camp. On liberation, in the Polish Navy in Great Britain. After the war, active in ex-combatant organisations, and from 1971 Chairman of the Polish Naval Association in Great Britain. He spent the last seven years of his life in the 'Antokol' Polish Residential Care Home, near London. Holder of the Polonia Restituta Order (V Class), the Cross of Valour and the Gold Cross of Merit with Swords.

102 Bogdan Walerian Michał Wroński (1908–1985) – 2nd Lieutenant in the Navy from 1930. In 1932, seconded to Fleet and Sub-unit Command in Gdynia (studying abroad). Promoted to the rank of Lieutenant Commander in 1938. According to OdB on 23 March 1939, artillery and armament administrator – seconded to Naval Command Services. Following the German assault on Poland, Naval Command in Warsaw was evacuated eastwards and Wroński made his way to France via Hungary. On 15 December 1939, reported to Polish Naval Command in Great Britain. Served on the destroyer ORP "Błyskawica" and in the rank of Naval Captain commanded the escort destroyer ORP "Ślązak" (for more information, see: B. Wroński, *Wspomnienia płyną jak okręty [Memories float like ships]*, London 1981). Settled in London after the war. Co-founder of the Polish Naval Association. During the period 1970–1975, Director of the Polish Institute and Gen. Sikorski Museum in London, then Deputy Chairman of the Board of the Institute during the period 1976-1980. From 1984, Minister of Military Affairs in the Polish Government-in-Exile in London. Holder of the Silver Cross of the Virtuti Militari Order, the Commander's Cross of the Polonia Restituta Order, the Naval Medal etc. Died suddenly in London, his ashes were laid to rest in the Polish Airmen's Cemetery in Newark.

London.

The staff of the printing company which I had taken over consisted of a book-keeper – Lionel Thomas Scott and a young trainee called Robert. The company's equipment included a modern German Heidelberg automatic printing machine, an old-style guillotine, and several sets of various moveable type fonts. I had never in my life seen such a machine and was not able to operate it. The former owner had promised to teach me how the printing press and the guillotine worked and that he would show me how to run the business. The company had many orders and while I was familiar with letter-setting I was still a novice at operating the new machine and printing. No wonder, then, that an accident took place at the beginning of my 'apprenticeship'.

In the course of printing, the owner stopped the machine to make some type adjustments. The safety cut-out was correctly set up but I did not know that it was faulty. When the owner finished making his adjustments he set the machine in motion and the lever began to move. Luckily, I realised in time that the cut-out system was not working and when the lever came close to my face, I moved backwards. Despite this, it hit me quite hard in the face and I fell over. The owner went white, he thought I was badly hurt. Luckily, the fact that I had ducked out of the way saved me from a serious injury – apart from falling on my back. And that was how I became familiar with the printing machine.

When Robert was called up, I advertised and found a new employee. Some time later, he, too, left and then I found an older person (of retirement age) who was well versed in the art of printing. I learned a great deal from him, so that I was able to run the print shop for several decades to come.

Both Scott and my elderly printer were with me when I retired. I sold the printing shop to an Indian and for several more years used to help him out – until he changed to a new method of printing. By this time my sight was getting worse and I had to retire completely. My acquaintance with Scott started when I took over the company in 1957 and our friendship has lasted to this day, even though I am now in a retirement home. Scott and my nephew deal with all my bank, tax and financial matters as my Powers of Attorney.

During my retirement, I devoted my time to work in various Polish Army organisations which had been established in the émigré community. When the Polish Army was disbanded and its members demobilized, all the cavalry regiments turned into Regimental Associations. This also included the 9th Lancers Regimental Association (the former Reconnaissance Unit of the 3rd [Infantry] Division named after the 9th Lancers Regiment), which I joined.

In keeping with a statement made by General Rudnicki that: "A Regimental Association shall last as long as at least one of its members continues to live", I can truthfully say that the Association continues to exist in my own person.

In Poland, too, there were Regimental Associations representing the old regiments. In Warsaw, for instance, there was an active 9th Lancers Regimental Association. Thanks to the initiative of Captain Włodzimierz Bernard[103] and the agreement of the authorities, a school in Radość was named after the 19th Wołyń Lancers Regiment, thus continuing pre-war traditions.

All the Regimental Association members kept in touch with each other and held various events and annual Regimental anniversary reunions. The 9th Lancers Regimental Association used to meet in the White Eagle Club in Balham, South London. One such event in 1978 was attended by a Mrs. Janina Rawska, who was looking for her friend – Zosia Tarnopolska – a member of our Association who had left the meeting for a moment. I happened to be close by and kept our guest company. It turned out that she was the Secretary of the Friends of Lwów Association and I, of course, had much to link me with Lwów!

After that first meeting, there were several more and I learned more about Janina's past. She had come to England with her son, using an illegally purchased passport. She had two sisters who lived outside Poland: the older sister in France, and a younger one who had been a member of the AK Polish Underground Resistance Army. She herself was suspected of spying and arrested but she was released from prison with the proviso that she was not considered to be innocent and that 'They' would find evidence to condemn her and would then bring her son up to be a good [Communist] citizen. This prompted her to buy a false passport and to leave for Great Britain. When Warsaw was being evacuated by the Germans, her husband had returned for a moment to their apartment to find something and a stray bullet had killed him.

Our acquaintanceship turned into friendship and during the 1970s (I cannot remember exactly when) but it was some two or three years after we met – that we decided to get married. At the time, my future wife worked in a Polish firm producing gramophone records and she lived with her son in her own house in the district of Chiswick. After our wedding, I moved into her house and her son went to live in her sister's house, a few streets away. Our marriage lasted eleven years. My wife suffered from a heart condition and she died in 1989. We had purchased a burial place in a cemetery in London by the Church of St. Andrzej

103 Włodzimierz Bernard (1912–2000) – 2nd Lieutenant – Reserves, in Cavalry Officers' Corps from 1938.

Bobola but, knowing how devoted Janina had been to her mother, I decided to arrange for her to be buried in her family grave in Podkowa Leśna, outside Warsaw. Since then I have visited Poland several times a year and recently at least once a year, in November.

15

1989: Return after fifty years

I went to Poland for the first time since the war with Sky Television, in 1989. They were making a special report with me to show what a Polish citizen, who had fought in September 1939 and throughout the Second World War and had spent half a century in exile, feels and how he reacts on his first return to Poland.

I keep in close contact with Poland and every year I attend meetings of the Foundation for the Preservation of the Polish Cavalry Tradition in Grudziądz, to which all the professional and reserve Officer Cadets belong. I also attend annual meetings of the 19th Wołyń Lancers Regimental Family, take part in Independence Day events and the Radość School's Anniversary Day in Warsaw. This close link with my beloved Poland is very important to me and I shall continue to maintain it as long as my strength and health allow.

For several decades, I have suffered from glaucoma and my state is very gradually getting worse. In 2010, there was a marked deterioration. Two women friends advised me that I should no longer try to cope on my own at home and they put me in the care of the 'Kolbe House' Residential Home in London, where I have been living ever since.

Epilogue

When I left Grudziądz after the splendid finish to my period in the Officer Cadet School, I never thought that I would ever return there. In 1989, with the "outbreak of a free Poland", my colleagues in Warsaw decided to organise a reunion of all the former Cavalry Officer Cadets from Grudziądz. They invited Karola Skowrońska, the director of the Grudziądz Municipal Library for help in the organisation of this event. For several months, she took part in the Organisation Committee's meetings in Warsaw where she "passed the test and proved" her knowledge of the cavalry. In 1995, she came to London to gather additional information on the subject in the Polish Institute and General Sikorski Museum and to meet the last living Grudziądz Officer Cadets. We were so impressed by this young, attractive and enthusiastic person that we unanimously voted to raise her to the rank of 'Honorary *Rotmistrz*'.

That first Reunion of the Regular Cavalry Officers in September 1989 led to further such events which, from year to year, increased in popularity. In 2013, the Foundation for the Preservation of the Polish Cavalry Tradition, led by Karola, organised the 25th Jubilee Convention of members of the Cavalry of the II Republic of Poland. It was attended by members of the Polish government and representatives of local authorities, as well as the Army, Voluntary Cavalry units and thousands of inhabitants of Grudziądz who filled the Market Square, the streets and the Vistula Parklands.

Grudziądz became famous throughout Poland and the world as the capital city of the Polish Cavalry.

Bibliography

ARCHIVAL SOURCES
Polish Library – POSK [Polish Social and Cultural Centre] in London
The B. O. Jeżewski Personnel Archives of the Polish Émigré Community

Polish Institute and Gen. Sikorski Museum [PISM] in London
Akta Oddziału Personalnego Sztabu NW [General Staff, Unit Personnel Records] (A.XII.27).

Akta z 17 września 1939 r. [Records from 17 September 1939]. (A.II.25).

Główne Kierownictwo Ewakuacji z Francji 1940 r. [Evacuation from France in 1940 – General Command Procedures] (A.IV.8/2).

Główny Oficer Łącznikowy przy Dowództwie Afryki Zachodniej [Chief Liaison Officer, West Africa Command] (A.XII.17).

Koło 9 Pułku Ułanów Małopolskich [9th Małopolski Lancers Regimental Club] (KOL. 438).

Referat Odznaczeń Gabinetu Naczelnego Wodza [Office of the Supreme Commander – Awards Division] (A.XII.85).

Samodzielny Wydział Spraw Zewnętrznych MON [Independent External Affairs Department – Ministry of National Defence] (A.XII.62).

Wołyńska Brygada Kawalerii – relacje z 1939 r. [Wołyń Cavalry Brigade – testimonies re 1939] (B.I.43).

Zarządzenie Prezydenta RP z 30 XII 1949 r. o nadaniu Krzyża Walecznych [Directive of the President of the Republic of Poland, dated 30.12.1949, relating to Award of Cross of Valour] (R 1391).

4 Dywizja Piechoty [4th Infantry Division] (A.VI.14).

The Polish Underground Movement Study Trust
Akta Stefana Bronisława Skupińskiego [Stefan Bronisław Skupiński's records] (TP2/1393).

PRIMARY SOURCES
Interview with *Rotmistrz* Tadeusz Bączkowski dated 31 July 2013

SECONDARY SOURCES: PUBLISHED WORKS AND RESEARCH MATERIAL

1. Dywizja Pancerna w walce. Praca zbiorowa [1st Armoured Division in Combat. Collective Work], Brussels 1947, reprint: Bielsko-Biała [2002].

10 Pułk Strzelców Konnych. Wspomnienia dedykowane pamięci wszystkich Dziesiątaków [10th Horse Rifles. Memoirs dedicated to the memory of all the 'Tenners'], commentary and editing: T. Skinder-Suchcitz, London 1995.

Anders W., *Bez ostatniego rozdziału. Wspomnienia z lat 1939–1946 [Without the Final Chapter. 1939-1945 Remembered]*, London 1989.

Biegański W., *Wojsko Polskie we Francji 1939–1940 [The Polish Army in France 1939-1940]*, Warsaw 1967.

Cud nad Tamizą. 25 lat Polskiego Ośrodka Społeczno-Kulturalnego w Wielkiej Brytanii [The Miracle on the Thames. 25th Anniversary of the Polish Social and Cultural Centre in GB], London 1989.

Czubiński A., *Historia Polski 1864–2001 [History of Poland 1864-2001]*, Wrocław 2008.

Czy wiesz kto to jest? [Do you know who this is?], ed. S. Łoza, Warsaw 1938.

Dowódcy pułku [Regimental Commanders], [in:] *Wielka Księga Kawalerii Polskiej 1918–1939. 19 Pułk Ułanów [The Big Book of the Polish Cavalry 1918-1939. The 19th Lancers Regiment]*, vol. 22, Warsaw 2012.

Dzieje Ułanów Jazłowieckich [The History of the Jazłowiecki Lancers], collective work, London 1988.

Eckert E., *Eksperyment. Polscy oficerowie w Afryce Zachodniej w latach 1941–1943 [An Experiment. Polish Officers in West Africa during the period 1941-1943]*, "PISM. Materiały – Dokumenty – Źródła – Archiwalia" [PISM. Material – Documents – Sources – Archives] 1988, file. 4.

Encyklopedia wojskowa [Military Encyclopaedia], ed. O. Laskowski, vol. 7, Warsaw 1939.

Englert J.L., Barbarski K., *Generał Maczek i żołnierze 1 Dywizji Pancernej [Gen. Maczek and the soldiers of the 1st Armoured Division]*, London 1992.

Ferenstein L., *Czarny naramiennik [Black Epaulette]*, Warsaw 1984.

Friszke A., *Życie polityczne emigracji [The Political Life of the Émigré Community]*, Warsaw 1999.

Grodziska K., *Polskie groby na cmentarzach Londynu [Polish Graves in London's Cemeteries]*, vol. 1, Kraków 1995.

Grodziska K., *Polskie groby na cmentarzach Londynu [Polish Graves in London's Cemeteries]*, vol. 2, Kraków 2001.

Habielski R., *Polski Londyn [Polish London]*, Wrocław 2000.

Jurga T., *Obrona Polski 1939 [The Defence of Poland 1939]*, Warsaw 1990.

Juszkiewicz R., Urbaniak A., *Dowódcy polskiego września [Commanders of Poland's September Campaign]*, Ciechanów 1989.

Kalendarium dziejów Polski od prehistorii do 2006 roku [A Calendar of Events – Poland from Prehistoric Times to 2006], ed. A. Chwalba, Kraków 2008.

Kondracki T., *Historia Stowarzyszenia Polskich Kombatantów w Wielkiej Brytanii 1946–1996 [The History of the Polish Ex-Combatants Association in Great Britain 1946-1996]*, London 1996.

Koszutski S., *Wspomnienia z różnych pobojowisk [Recollections from Various Fields of Battle]*, London 1972.

Kozłowski E., *Wojsko Polskie 1936–1939. Próby modernizacji i rozbudowy [The Polish Army 1936-1939. Attempts at Modernisation and Enlargement]*, Warsaw 1974.

Kryska-Karski T., *Materiały do historii Wojska Polskiego [The Polish Army – Supplementary Material]*, no. 1–20, London 1982–1986 (publ. by the author).

Kukawski L., *Historia pułku [History of the Regiment]*, [in:] *Wielka Księga Kawalerii Polskiej 1918–1939. 19 Pułk Ułanów [The Big Book of the Polish Cavalry 1918-1939. The 19th Lancers Regiment]*, vol. 22, Warsawa 2012.

Kukawski L., Leżeński C., *O kawalerii polskiej XX wieku [The Polish Cavalry in the 20th Century]*, Wrocław 1991.

Kukawski L., Tym J.S., *Historia Centrum Wyszkolenia Kawalerii [History of the Cavalry Training Centre]*, [in:] *Wielka Księga Kawalerii Polskiej 1918–1939. Centrum Wyszkolenia Kawalerii [The Big Book of the Polish Cavalry 1918-1939. The 19th Lancers Regiment]*, vol. 47, Warsaw 2013.

Krzeczunowicz K., *Ułani księcia Józefa. Historia 8 Pułku Ułanów ks. Józefa Poniatowskiego 1784–1945 [Prince Józef's Lancers. History of the 8th (Prince J. Poniatowski) Lancers Regiment 1784-1945]*, London 1960.

Łukomski G., *Ułan i strażnik kawaleryjskiej pamięci. Rotmistrz Zygmunt Godyń 1910–1979 [A Lancer and the Guardian of Cavalry Traditions. Captain-of-Horse Zygmunt Godyń 1910-1979]*, Poznań – Warsaw – London 2015.

Maczek S., *Od podwody do czołga. Wspomnienia wojenne 1918–1945 [From the Horse Levy to the Tank. Wartime memoirs 1918-1945]*, Edinburgh 1961.

Mała encyklopedia wojskowa [Small Military Encyclopaedia], ed. O. Laskowski, vol. 1, Warsaw 1930.

Nowa encyklopedia powszechna PWN [The New Universal PWN Encyclopaedia], editor-in-chief D. Kalisiewicz, vol. 5: *P–S*, Warsaw 1997.

Nurek M., *Gorycz zwycięstwa. Los Polskich Sił Zbrojnych na Zachodzie po II wojnie światowej 1945–1949 [The Bitterness of Victory. The Fate of the Polish Armed Forces in the West after the Second World War, 1945-1949]*, Gdańsk 2009.

Pierwsza Dywizja Pancerna. Polegli na polu chwały w drodze do Polski [First Armoured Division. They Died in Battle En Route to Poland], collective work, London 1964.

Polskie Siły Zbrojne w II wojnie światowej [Polish Armed Forces in the Second World War], vol. 1: *Kampania wrześniowa 1939 [September 1939 Campaign]*, part 1: *Polityczne i wojskowe położenie Polski przed wojną [Poland's Political and Military Situation before the War]*, London 1951.

Przybyszewski A., *9. Pułk Ułanów Małopolskich 1809–1947 [9th Małopolski Lancers Regiment 1809-1947]*, Radomyśl Wielki 2011.

Radomski J.A., *Demobilizacja Polskich Sił Zbrojnych na Zachodzie w latach 1945–1951 [Demobilisation of the Polish Armed Forces in the West 1945-1951]*, Kraków 2009.

Rocznik Oficerski 1932 [Officers' Yearbook 1932], Ministerstwo Spraw Wojskowych Biuro Personalne [Personnel Department, Ministry of Military Affairs], Warsaw 1932.

Rudnicki K., *Na polskim szlaku [On the Polish Trail]*, London 1952.

Rumuński azyl. Losy Polaków 1939–1945 [Romanian Asylum. The Fate of Poles 1939-1945], ed. A. Wancerz-Gluza, Warsaw 2009.

Rybka R., Stepan K., *Awanse oficerskie w Wojsku Polskim 1935–1939 [Promotion of Officers in the Polish Army 1935-1939]*, Kraków 2003.

Rybka R., Stepan K., *Rocznik Oficerski 1939 [Officers' Yearbook 1939. As at 23 March 1939]*, Kraków 2006.

Rycerze, Infułat i Pastor, czyli wojenne wspomnienia spod Krzyża Południa [The Monsignor and the Pastor, or Wartime Memories from under the Southern Cross], red. A. Krzychylkiewicz, A. Romanowicz, Warsaw 2013.

Schweizer L., *Wojna bez legendy [War without a Legend]*, Kirkcaldy 1943.

Siemaszko Z.S., *Generał Anders w latach 1892–1942 [Gen. Anders during the period 1892-1942]*, London – Warsaw 2012.

Siemaszko Z.S., *I co dalej? (1945–1948) [And what next? 1945-1948]*, London – Warsaw 2016.

Skiba A., *Boje 19 Pułku Ułanów Wołyńskich w kampanii wrześniowej [The Battles of the 19th Wołyń Lancers Regiment in the September Campaign]*, London 1971.

Strumph-Wojtkiewicz S., *Wbrew rozkazowi. Wspomnienia oficera prasowego 1939–1945 [Against orders. Memoirs of an Army Press Spokesman 1939-1945]*, Warsaw 1961.

Suchcitz A., *"Non omnis moriar ... Polacy na londyńskim cmentarzu Brompton [Non omnis moriar ... Poles in London's Brompton Cemetery]*, Warsaw 1992.

Suchcitz A., *Stankiewicz Ludwik*, [in:] *Polski słownik biograficzny [Polish Biographical Dictionary]*, vol. XLII/2, file. 173, ed. K. Staniszewska, M. Starczewski, Warsaw – Kraków 2003.

Szymczyk D., *Zbigniew Makowiecki w obozach jenieckich Wehrmachtu [Zbigniew Makowiecki* in the Wehrmacht's POW Camps], Łambinowicki Rocznik Muzealny 2014, vol. 37.

Śp. rtm. Tadeusz Bączkowski [The Late Captain-of-Horse Tadeusz Bączkowski], Komunikat Fundacji na Rzecz Tradycji Jazdy Polskiej, 2015, R. 25, no. 50.

Święcicki M., Pasażer na gapę. Opowiadania [Free Rider. Tales], London 1983.

Tomaszewski S., Szkic historyczny 9 Pułku Ułanów Małopolskich [Brief History of the 9th Małopolski Lancers Regiment], [in:] 9 Pułk Ułanów Małopolskich [9th Małopolski Lancers Regiment], ed. Z. Godyń, Edinburgh 1947.

Warszawa nad Tamizą. Z dziejów polskiej emigracji politycznej po drugiej wojnie światowej [Warsaw-on-the-Thames. The Polish Émigré Community after the Second World War], ed. A. Friszke, Warsaw 1994.

Wawer Z, Pawłowski E., Polskie Siły Zbrojne na obczyźnie [Polish Armed Forces in Exile], [in:] Wojsko Polskie w II wojnie światowej [The Polish Army in the Second World War], ed. E. Pawłowski, Z. Wawer, Warsaw 2005.

Who's Who 1954, London 1954.

Wroński B., Wspomnienia płyną jak okręty [Memories Float like Ships], London 1981.

Zubrzycki J., Polish Immigrants in Britain, The Hague 1956.

Zuziak J., 3. Dywizja Piechoty Wojska Polskiego we Francji w 1940 roku [The 3rd Infantry Division of the Polish Army in France in 1940], Toruń 2001.

Żołnierze Generała Maczka [General Maczek's Soldiers], research and editing Z. Mieczkowski, in association with S. Wyganowski, W. Żakowski, Warsaw – London 2003.

JOURNALS AND UNIT BULLETINS

"Dziewiątak. Biuletyn Koła Pułkowego 9 Pułku Ułanów Małopolskich" ['The Niner'. 9th Małopolski Lancers Regiment, Bulletin of the Regimental Association] 1951, R. VI, no. 33.

"Komunikat Fundacji na Rzecz Tradycji Jazdy Polskiej" [Communiqué of the Foundation for the Preservation of the Polish Cavalry Tradition] 1991–2015.

"Piechota 1939–1945" [Infantry 1939-1945] 1970–1974, file: 1–17 (1972, file 9/10; 1973, file 12).

"Ułan Wołyński. Czasopismo Stowarzyszenia Rodzina 19 Pułku Ułanów Wołyńskich" [The Wołyń Lancers. Journal of the 19th Wołyń Lancers Regimental Family Association] 2015, issue 55.

Index of People